FOR LOVE OF MY LIFE

FOR

LOVE

OF MY LIFE

CHRISTMAS IN PARIS

DEUX FOIS

SHERRIE FORD

MIGLIOR PRESS • ATHENS, GEORGIA

Published by Miglior Press
Athens, Georgia

www.migliorpress.com

ISBN 978-0-9836484-1-3

Printed in the United States of America

First Edition

For all the people
in what a friend told me
is my "suitcase heart"

CYNICISM

I once saw a sunset
so vivid and warm that I swore it was perfect.
I once had a lover;
I'm not sure if I'll recover,
but I know it was worth it.
Then, last night in the car,
the falling raindrops looked like stars
at some incalculable speed.
Then later, my friends said, "Good to see you again."
This is a home to me.

So I wrote a song, and I called it "The Love of My Life."
Said, "Don't be gone long;" it now sings me to sleep every night.

And I never learned a lesson looking at my own reflection,
but sometimes it seems useful,
so I loosen my heart strings in high hopes
of starting to find something truthful.

Cynicism isn't wisdom;
it's a lazy way to say that you've been burned.
It seems, if anything,
you'd be less certain after everything you ever learned.

Theodore Hilton

CONTENTS

PREFACE

I had been taking French at Dell City High School in Dell City, Oklahoma, when my dad was assigned to a NATO base a few hours northwest of Paris. It was 1960, I was thirteen, and it was really just luck that I arrived in France with a little bit of *comment allez-vous.* I then went to an international boarding school in France and spent the next two years living in dorms away from home. I was at an impressionable age, and those high school years in France shaped my teenage self and, to some extent, the rest of my young life. I went on to major in French as an undergraduate, and I taught French at a two-year college while I got my Ph.D.

I still hold on to memories of the time our family spent in France. I remember my dad taking me to Paris once a month, first to get my braces on, later to have them adjusted. He always made me feel grown up by letting me do all the talking when we got on and off the Metro and while we were looking for the dentist's office. I remember glimpses of Paris from these visits, but what stays with me most is the sense of confidence and self-assurance I had in myself as a navigator and savvy, would-be Parisian girl.

In the end, France has little to do with the life and career I've built. After my family left, I didn't have another chance to return to France until 2003. In my day-to-day life, only occasionally am I even conscious of the fact that I can speak and read a little French. It always makes me think how strange it is that few others in my life share this ability. Yet, when it occurs to me, I feel enriched by a special, personal knowledge of the language, the place, and the people.

France has always provided this other identity, almost a past-life. This is the part of myself that was forged as a thirteen-year-old with braces and strengthened as a young woman dividing my time between literary theory and teaching. It's my past; the whole study of French history, language, literature, and culture was a huge part of my young life. So when I had a chance to go back to Paris in my late fifties, it felt like an unexpected opportunity. I guess the cliché of "you're not getting any younger" inspired me to reconsider what good it does not to do things. So I got to reopen my personal dialogue with France and begin a new chapter in my life.

Going back to Paris has the power of bringing the past into the contemporary, giving me an adult perspective on what I saw as a teenager. It is a very different view. I was recently looking for the top of Montmartre when I suddenly stumbled upon Le Moulin Rouge. It was just a little windmill. In my memory, however, it had been magnified beyond reality. When I went with my mom and dad it had been something else entirely. Then, the naked women dancing had just shocked me to my teeth.

That first trip back, in 2003, was with Gwendolyn Galsworth, who had just staged a magnificent conference in Amsterdam on visual factory. I had presented on the cultural side of manufacturing. When Gwen said, "Let's just go to Paris for a few days on the way back and reward ourselves," I thought, "Gosh, what a concept." That finally broke down the wall in my mind of "you can't just go back on your own" because we were doing exactly that.

On that first trip, I had lots of travel miles from my job, so I didn't even have to buy a ticket. My pleasure in just being there was, simply, extreme. That first night, we walked down from the hotel to Notre Dame, purely to see Notre Dame before sunset. It was a Friday evening, and there were hundreds, I would almost say thousands, of skateboarders. They were going in this big loop that brought them to the front of Notre Dame. It wasn't chaotic, and police were present, making sure everybody was safe. It was just this breathtaking social event. I felt updated on what the world was doing. I really felt I had had no idea before. Now, when I go back, I always see something like that going on somewhere in Paris, and the experience has that same, eye-opening effect on me.

I left Paris that trip having found a base, a hotel that I could use as a place to go back to every visit. I also caught Gwendolyn's contagious enthusiasm for finding her way back to the past. She had lived in Paris in her younger years and knew how to walk everywhere; we didn't even need the Metro. She remembered going to Mariage Frères, a famous tea-importer with a restaurant, and it became our favorite spot for Sunday brunch.

Later I took Theo, one of my sons, back to Paris with me. I took him because I wanted to show him what I had discovered through Gwen. That trip showed me a lot, mainly what Paris looked like from his point of view.

We went to Mariage Frères to have brunch; he told me he found the whole thing extremely decadent. He meant all of Paris, not just that place. I really enjoyed getting to know the Puritan, political side of Theo on that trip. He just wanted to know where the anarchists were.

We found the place at the Cimetière du Père-Lachaise where Jim Morrison is buried, and we saw the wall where the anarchists of one era were shot, but that's as close as we came to satisfying his quest on our first attempt. So he felt disappointed.

Then, later we were at a flea market, and some really unusual-looking people came our way and caught his eye, and he turned around and started following them. He asked them where the anarchists were and, to my surprise, they told him. So we went to a bookstore they had directed him to, and he picked out some things, but they wouldn't take my credit card, likely because they were anarchists. Anyway, I didn't have the cash necessary to trade with them.

Through my very idealistic son, I got to know that political dimension of Paris. In fact, in the years since that trip I have gone back to reread French history, and I discovered much more revolutionary spirit in that past than in ours. Unfortunately, Theo and I didn't get to strike that chord then. Now I would know where to take him. I know where the fates of Louis XVI, Marie Antoinette, and others really played out, and I love to share that knowledge. I find I'm even surprised by how disappointed I am that you can't really go to the Bastille now.

I would try to get people to go back to Paris with me after my trip with Theo. They would want to, but couldn't. So I just wound up coming on my own. Now I don't really want to be with anybody else; I want to be on my own because I know exactly what I want to do with my time in Paris. I can sleep when I want to sleep, and it just might be all day. Conversely, I can get completely lost in a search for something and spend days looking or just meandering. I don't think I can quite see others getting on my agenda. ("What! We're in Paris and we're going to sleep all day?" or "We're going to walk? You don't want to go on the Metro? Your feet aren't bleeding?")

I now go every other year, at Christmas time. I haven't noticed it so much in past years, but this past Christmas at home, I really missed being there. I thought about it almost every day from mid-December to early January. I found myself wondering: "Is that shop still there, the one that had the pretty rings?" "Is that lady that I bought the heart-shaped paperweights from still there? Did she miss me this year?" I had to stop and laugh at myself. Of course, Paris doesn't need me the same way I've come to need it, but it's comforting to imagine the city waiting for my next visit.

SHERRIE FORD

2005 TRIP

December 18, 2005
Paris, rue des Écoles

The sun is bright now, but it will too soon be gone, and I am only just now revived enough to venture out. I set out, taking a different street from past visits, and realize that this is, indeed, the Latin Quarter.

I have to pause almost immediately to take in a scene that you would never find in America, not even in the most intellectual university town. A boy of twelve or thirteen is in deep conversation with an older man, perhaps his father or uncle. They are in front of a closed bookstore with display windows featuring radical philosophers, titles on politics and economics. Even from the street, I can see dialectical assertions of Heidegger's persistent influence. Next door to the bookshop is an artsy cinema featuring old American films, now featuring Shirley McClain and Jack Lemmon in *The Apartment*.

I am surprised that something from my own youth could now be regarded by the French youth as an historic aesthetic experience. This reopens what will probably be the theme of these two weeks: time passing, time caught off guard or, more appropriately, past guard. In all honesty, this week is making me miss being young, and, of course, taking that youth for granted. In this particular moment, walking by groups of young people produces the same sensation as passing through business class on your way out of the airplane. You see the detritus—or, even worse, casual rejection—of the finer elements of luxury. You follow in the wake of those who do not have to endure overly cramped seats, overly packaged meals, blankets too thin, screens shared by the masses, a flight without hot towels to refresh one's stressed and delicate skin. Anyway, youth was a first-class journey, and now one is boarded daily to the unenvied rows.

I continue, passing a massive building with a sign reading "École Polytechnique." The building must date to the 1800s and is covered with vines. The surrounding grounds appear dipped in gold from leaves that still have not fallen so late in the year. Children play in an unexpected playground.

I stop in a café. As I sip a white wine recommended by the waiter, I am thankful it's not cold and rainy. Tourists of many nationalities review maps. I'm secretly glad that I left mine in the room, to study in private after sundown. Right now, the thing I covet most in the world is an apartment in the Latin Quarter. I want friends and a place to live as if I belonged. From such an apartment, I could do everything without a second thought. No need for maps, vocabulary, or my persistent fear of taking the Metro. After wistfully drifting through the possibilities, I decide it's time to return to the hotel.

ↄ

A few hours later, I step out into rue Monge a new woman. I am freshly bathed, shampooed, and napped. I head left immediately in hopes that the *marché* on Mouffetard will still be open. It is. My first purchase—bread and cheese to cover unexpected hunger pangs that will be sure to come at the least convenient time. I know only these few blocks and streets, and I would prefer not to be driven to eating, in desperation, junk food from Asian delis.

I end the day eating at La Petite Périgourdine, pasta with *foie gras* and mushrooms. Very tasty. Smokers tap ash onto the floor. The day has a definite Sunday atmosphere. It's relaxed, lazy even, yet I don't feel I'm missing anything regarding the margins I am here to experience. I read Theroux's *Blinding Light* with his usual permission to stir up cruelties. He must have suffered enormous disappointments as a boy, enormous ridicule, enormous standards set by someone equally refusing to acknowledge that such things have sliding scales when it comes to psychic torture. I love his books and wonder why I am so attracted to them. *The Sea.* Amazing.

December 19, 2005
Hotel Monge

I woke up and passed the morning with a surprising feeling of being weighed down or handicapped. It's nearly 2:50 p.m., and I'm still in my room. Unlike yesterday, today is rainy and cold. It's hard to stop my mind from moving over the boulders of my life. That's the general lay of the land, huge rocks. I'm not saying they aren't beautiful. Still, I leave the hotel room with a sense of relief.

‌❧

I am relaxing at a *salon de thé* near the hotel. I have forgotten my colorful pens. I have been walking for the last two hours, touring St. Chapelle and La Conciergerie, two places near Notre Dame that I'd missed before. Seeing the large, stone half circle that was a washing place for clothes in the Cour des Femmes brings characters from the stories to life. After all, it was perhaps the only place that women prisoners could be outside.

December 20, 2005
Bergamote

Only I can manage to have a full set of colored pens and then leave the room without the right color to make these entries. This will be unreadable.

I am at Côté Bergamote—a place to have a lunch of healthy herbed dishes and experiments with wine. The restaurant is completely full at the moment. The clientele are mostly—or entirely, except for me—French. Some children. Some sweethearts. Some girlfriends. I choose the recommended *entrée, plat, dessert,* and *salade—crumble de pomme & poire*—and the recommended wine experiment. The wine is unbelievably sweet, herbal, and delicious. In fact, I think it is the best white wine I have ever tasted. I added dessert this time because the menu indicates "garnished with violets."

The idea today was to walk all the way down to St. Germaine Boulevard and on to Les Invalides. Of course, I had wanted to visit Napoleon's tomb. As it happened, however, the walk led to this restaurant first. What a find. I am so glad I am able to push the boundaries of what I know a bit more each day.

At first on this trip, I wasn't sure I could make it. I feel less trepidation today, however, than I did on Sunday and Monday. Even as the day continues, my feelings about the trip are getting better. At first I really felt that I had made a mistake in coming: in coming for so long, in coming alone, and in coming at a potentially bad time for my company and my life. These thoughts—and, probably, eating a panini from a sidewalk stand—made me violently ill the first night. The episode, which I have thus far omitted for the sake of first impressions and general morale, was truly horrible and terrifying. The room seemed to be actually spinning, and my stomach felt like the enemy. I lay still, eyes closed, till the spinning stopped, and learned by trial and error that if I opened them again, the spinning increased in intensity. Was it the basil on the panini? Was it something more sinister? I faced the prospect of many days abed, blue, semi-sick, effectively blind, with reading novels as my only rescue. At that moment, I had felt the whole trip was about to fall apart, and my sense of independence with it. Now that the episode is in the past, I think I can admit that, to some degree, I've been battling that fear ever since and, very slowly, winning.

For example, only two days ago, I was afraid to walk beyond the immediate surroundings of the hotel. A new anxiety about directions is surprising. I did not expect to confront the degree of helplessness that has come, I suppose, with aging.

I realize my eyesight has become weak, even with contacts. Also, it is partly impaired while writing because the skin beneath my eyes is so loose and baggy that it intrudes on the field of sight. If I pull the side of my face taut, the page re-emerges. It's effective, but hardly efficient. My memory, though, is the major concern. Venturing out becomes a trek into an unknown, even with maps and signs everywhere.

Yet, despite it all, I wind up here, seated in Bergamote, where all these concerns seem to vanish. Here, a combination of tradition and innovation really works. I've been in many little corner restaurants in Paris, but this is the first to reflect a recent renovation. It has an air of being very youthful and healthy (or, at least, it is one of the few places where they segregate the smokers). Most of all, it is flavorful in ways that other places aren't. After entering a typical hooded front door, you find small tables, chalkboard menus, mirrors on the wall. One wall is entirely devoted to a display of potted herbs. Something you'd find in a dedicated, stylish kitchen. Here, however, it seems effortless, as if everybody takes the power of fresh herbs in the food and wine for granted. I wish I could buy a bottle of this ambience.

&

On another note: the beret is ever stylish in Paris. I wonder if I'll buy one.

&

Later—many miles later, in fact—I'm at an establishment called Breakfast in America, which turns out to be an American-style roadside diner. The waiters are clearly American. There's ketchup and mustard on every table and red leather booths. There's even an NFL game on the TV. This could be The Grill, the longtime casual dining spot at home in Athens.

December 21, 2005
Hotel Monge

Too tired to comment. I used my time at the restaurant today to read *The Herald Tribune* instead of writing about the day, but here is a list to hopefully prompt a future entry:

- I saw St. Eustache Cathedral. There, Cardinal Richelieu was baptized, and Louis XIV had his first communion. It's now very run-down and neglected.
- I walked to 68 Champs-Élysées and found a giant, white Ferris wheel, with the Eiffel Tower in the view beyond.
- There's less fear today.
- I found a Chinese lady dressed in my exact same outer wear: black coat with a fur-trimmed hood, purple bag, purple gloves. Her daughter pointed me out to her mother.
- I can find my two favorite restaurants now, both healthy.
- I can find a P. O. now to buy stamps.
- The phone card is nearly used up.
- All seems to be collapsing back at work. I fear it will all make Paris a sort of Last Supper.
- I lay in bed after the hot bath this morning for nearly an hour. Hair wet, room not entirely cold enough, the street very loud, and my mind frozen. It felt for some time as if I might not get out of bed today. Another person(ality) eventually made me, and so I dressed and went out into the city.

December 22, 2005
Desert Rose

I am now at Desert Rose—an Arabic teahouse on rue Blanche. I'm taking a well-deserved break as I climb my way to Montmartre and Sacré-Coeur. I've walked so very far today that I may be forced to brave the fangs of the Metro. How I dread getting lost and not knowing how to find the right train. I have been walking non-stop for two hours now, although somewhat slowly at times. I've had to pause to study the map, stare at a number of grand edifices, and read plaques commemorating the places where national heroes were shot dead by the SS. I'd gotten so worn down and thirsty that when I came upon the "Petit Thé" and "Desert Rose" signs, I gave in quickly.

The other clients here are young—a girl and a boy. I'm guessing they are Egyptian. The waiter is also a young man, perhaps in his twenties. They speak French, but with a marked accent. Water pipes bubble. I realize this place could be straight out of Mahfouz's *Cairo Trilogy*. In fact, the whole place could have been taken from Egypt in the '20s. There are candles everywhere, and brocades upholster narrow divans. Sheer orange curtains cover the windows, and photos of a man sitting in desert sand occupy a prominent place on the wall. The room is heavily perfumed, perhaps from the candles. A boom box blares American semi-rap.

My tea is served in a silver pot with curves and a big black handle. The waiter pours it into a tiny glass with gold trim. I give it a moment to cool slightly.

The tea, a mint-honey flavor, has a light taste, but is somehow thick at the same time. It is delicious. What a delightful surprise.

❧

It was another morning of giving in to inertia. Though I woke up at eight, I didn't leave the hotel until half-past one. I can't imagine life being this slow and immobile at home. Absolutely nothing sets my agenda for the day here, except the ten o'clock closing of the *petit déjeuner*. I truly considered skipping it today. Even that. Yet, after the usual croissant and coffee, I just came back upstairs and didn't even bother with a bath. Just back to bed. An hour, maybe more, not sleeping, trying not to think too much, waiting for thoughts and stress from home to abate and Paris to sink in. For a moment I toyed with the idea of some sort of depression, but quickly embraced it as a pure state of "crashing," whereby time seems to both collapse and expand.

Time collapsing: paying no attention to a clock or what I might be missing. Paying no attention to anyone else's schedule.

Time expanding: It seems there is no limit to what to do or think or pay attention to. Lack of structure allows absolutely everything surrounding me to ooze into my thoughts. Regretfully, this often produces a twinge of anxiety or guilt.

Time collapsing: I am not as young as I used to be. I panic, thinking if I close my eyes for even a minute, when I open them again I'll be blind. I'll be paralyzed. It seems that time has become just one more minute.

Time expanding: I feel thrown deeply into the past by walking upon the ground of a country whose history is so engrained in my own: mine and my country's. *Liberté, egalité, fraternité.* These connections of time and place give me perspective. The current political situation seems a joke. I wonder how Bush gained power, how he got anyone to take him seriously. I remember Pinter's comments on how Bush has effectively hypnotized the world. Bush seems an anachronism here, dismissible. Meanwhile, I have the feeling of touching, of being part of, something more profound. I now have gotten my bearings, looking at such deep, deep past at the Ile de la Cité, settled by tribes hundreds of years BC. I then take on the stylized half-streets that maze me onward and sideways into one time zone after another. I pass this church from the twelfth century, then that one from the seventh. Then there are many signs of Napoleon III in the 1800s, he who put in the wide boulevards, then took what might otherwise have become space for larger apartments and made the grand buildings of *l'État*.

The tea is truly amazing.

Two young girls come in, kiss the waiter, and begin chatting. No one orders anything. They're all sucking on the same pipe. Is there something in the pipe that makes them speak so loudly?

The semi-rap has me bouncing my head and tapping my toe. Is time expanding or collapsing now? Regardless, I am way too old to be in here, yet the tea is exquisite, and the smoke from the pipe is not insufferable. In fact, the smell is strangely aromatic and sweet. Why is that?

December 23, 2005
Across the street from Notre Dame, in the garden of the Polytech

A vert your eyes while I list the following "next time bring" items: baggies for the long walks (to save half-sandwiches), toothbrush for the purse, a whole bottle of Aleve, more socks, Band-Aids, packets of Tide, Splenda, toothpicks, floss, wipes, earplugs, CD player with natural sounds.

Don't bring: but one lipstick, the old camera, but three pairs of nylon underwear (wash nightly).

Otherwise I think I did a good job of bringing attractive but comfortable clothes this time. (I shrink away from being the American tourist in jeans or sweatpants at national monuments.) Additionally, I brought only one pair of shoes, hand wash, packets of Kleenex, cold-symptom suppressants, and Swiss army knife to cut cheese and fruits in the room. Not bad, and, with the above, I could be perfectly prepared.

 confused

I am now in Les Tuileries gardens, seated in a lawn chair before a very skimpy fountain. At the moment I wish they had a pageant about Joséphine Bonaparte here. I would love to walk in the Tuileries gardens and see her show up for a stroll. The day started out warm and sunny, so I left my overcoat and gloves in the room, but now, only an hour later, the warmth and sun have disappeared. Now my fingers are stiff from cold. My arthritic thumb sends up excruciating pain just holding this pen, let alone making it move to write. What follows is therefore to be read with a little extra appreciation.

Everyone has been very friendly and helpful. I love it when French people stop me and ask where to find things like *"oiseaux comme il faut"*—I am sure she asked for proper birds. My reply gave away that she'd mistaken me for a countryman. I felt disappointed, too.

∾

I am now headed to Musée de l'Orangerie, home of impressionists even more important than those who are in d'Orsay, or so they say. Actually, it was specifically Damian at Montmartre—who drew my portrait last night, a whole story in itself—who scorned the Louvre and sends me to l'Orangerie—which is closed for renovation. It's supposed to re-open in 2006. I had hoped to put off the Louvre until after Christmas, but I'm now at Restaurant le Grande Louvre, where I've come because it was close by and I remembered they serve large cups of decaf coffee. A bottle of water and a cup of coffee have cost me seven euros (that is *nine* dollars). But, hey, art and history and being a stranger all add value to the experience. I'd spend more, for sure. Especially for decaf. I ended up paying dearly for the two pots of tea yesterday. At four this morning, I was still awake, and, consequently, soon I'll have read all of the books I brought. I also missed *le petit déjeuner* entirely, hence the deep sensation of pleasure I feel with this cup before me, steaming, with a half an inch of foam on top. The *eau minérale* Vittel, meanwhile, is already gone.

∾

On my way to l'Orangerie I stopped at the Ferris wheel to get my bearings and decided to ride it after all (only eight euros). They paired me with another solo lady tourist who turned out to be a library science professor from the United States. She chattered the entire time, and I missed taking several pictures. I had especially wanted to take a picture of Montmartre from that vantage point. It looked so separate from the rest of Paris. There, on the hill, was the amazing Sacré-Cœur, which I climbed to yesterday after Desert Rose and lit a candle for my company. The artist who drew my portrait shortly before I went into the basilica told me that doing so would bring luck and make a wish come true.

His name, he said, was Damian. I had stumbled into the artists' square that Juniper had described to me. I was looking over the displays of four or five of them, admiring their skill, when I hear someone call out, "Madame! I want to draw your face."

"No thanks, just looking."

"Let me show you a brief sketch. Then you decide," he insisted.

Well, he got the hair right. Nothing else really looks like me. The value of the episode was in the conversation we made as he worked. I realized then that I had not had one long dialogue since the beginning of the trip, let alone in French. We discussed Paris, history, art, my children and grandchildren, and why I am here by myself. I was as fluent as I needed to be. His English was also good enough to help me with a word or two. He even explained the essence of *fraternité,* which I'd sort of lost the meaning of.

I left the square with a feeling of serendipitous accomplishment. It was similar to yesterday when I arrived at the top of rue Blanche to find Pigalle and the Moulin Rouge, to my surprise.

Sooner or later, the pieces seem to fall into place. This would not have happened if I'd come with anyone else or if I only had a week to spend. Who would have walked nearly eight miles with me today and then up a giant hill of twisting, cobblestone lanes?

Yet I have also found traveling alone has a definite downside. It was very dark on the descent, and a surge of panic hit me. *Don't be scared don't be scared don't be scared.* Miss Chatty on the Ferris wheel said we're safe around the clock, inasmuch as "they don't allow guns here." I did take some comfort in that. My map is now nearly wrung out from my clutching, reading, re-reading, and re-clutching till I got past the vacant streets and back into the bobbing safe haven of the last-minute, Christmas-shopping throngs. From there, I found my way back to the healthy restaurant with relative ease. Salon des Tartes is the name of the place. I had an extremely large salad and a big pot of Earl Grey (mistake) and, yes, a rhubarb tart.

☙

I heard my dad's voice today very distinctly as he used to say at the door after I'd gone to bed, "*Bonne nuit*"—it sounded like bone wheat. Bone wheat. In his young voice, as if I were fifteen and he were forty-three.

It is half-past five in the evening now and the sun is gone—it began to disappear an hour ago, but now it has finally set, and I am glad to be at a restaurant on rue Monge. I was beginning to feel desperate as many of the restaurants that I've been passing as I walk to and fro on expeditions (at times just lost) are closed, business lights out. It is only two days till Christmas, so I should not be surprised. My waiter just now assures me that several will be open on Christmas, on rue des Écoles and up and down St. Germaine Boulevard. Why I picked this one out of those restaurants still open tonight: it is dark, large enough to have four little tables with no ashtray, and the menu doesn't have hamburgers and fries. This is not to suggest that fries are a serious problem for me, but there is already a McDonald's on St. Germaine Boulevard, and the only other large place here seems set up as some kind of direct competition. Also, the menu outside said "Lasagna" with a green salad, and I was hungry after a walk of five hours, give or take, including a few small breaks for writing and shopping. The *marché* at Mouffetard was open this morning. I went there for fruit but wound up starting the gift search, which continued in earnest once I saw l'Orangerie was closed.

Where do these Parisian restaurants get their sound tracks? "Volare" to the Stones to rapping to Elvis.

How did the waiter know I wanted decaf? I am gray-haired, American, and sitting alone in the non-smoking, or rather the "no smoking at these few, tiny tables" section. Any of the above should be a dead giveaway. I hold my hideous thumb joints against the hot cup. The pharmacist sold me an over-the-counter medication for angina (of all conditions) because of its anti-inflammatory properties. He also told me to put the hair dryer on the joint to help with pain. We'll see.

Also I must record that earlier I saw a pair of calf-high boots made of deep-purple leather in the window of a shop just off boulevard Saint-Germain. I so wanted those boots. If my company survives this crisis and I ever get to come back here with a credit card that means business, I am going to buy the future edition of those boots.

December 24, 2005
Chez Léon, boulevard Saint-Germain

Since my first delightful experience there, the restaurant Bergamote has proved frustratingly elusive. It closed just ten minutes before I arrived today, after I'd planned all morning to go there for lunch. It closed early for the holiday, apparently. About one block away, on boulevard Saint-Germain, I am instead dining (when there is wine, you dine, not eat) at Chez Léon, a Brussels-cuisine establishment; I deduce this means *moules* or "mussels" after observing that everyone has a little crock-pot full of them. So, soon, shall I.

Some relief has come for the joint pain now that I've had two doses of the anti-inflammatory recommended by the chemist. I was doubtful, but it has definitely taken the edge off—I can open a door now without wanting to howl.

The wine is a glass of muscadet. I chose it because I thought it might be sweeter, but it doesn't really taste very good, nor did the choice from last night. Only the divine flavor of the wine at Bergamote is worthy of the overall goals of this trip. Overall goals—that's not really right. There are no goals here. Or perhaps there's only one: to see what happens. Oops, I must go, as a yellow crock-pot of mussels and a steel bowl of French fries are now here.

෮

Much later in the day: The mussels in a cream base were really good after all. The French bread, soaked in the remaining broth, heightened my whole sense of triumph over despair at the time.

I was so pleased with myself that I forgot to ask, as I paid the bill, which way to the toilet. A mile or two later I realized this error and was forced to retreat to a McDonald's. While access is allowed to the restrooms, they are dark and very unpleasant. I applauded myself a second time for remembering to carry packets of Kleenex.

Now I am at a place where I think I have found a waiter who is kind, or at least sympathetic. It is virtually next door to the hotel, thus always overlooked. Last night I stood outside the door reading the menu as I was about to go in for the night, when the waiter opened the door and greeted me. He invited me in to an empty room of one long banquette with five facing chairs and an assortment of small tables and chairs here and there. I said no, but asked about Christmas Eve and Christmas. He replied that, yes, they would be open both days. Today at the same end-of-day time, I stopped by just to ask how late.

Now I am seated here with the onion soup and a glass of Prestige Bordeaux, which came recommended. He also recommended the steak—he's swears it's tender, even the best. Now the waiter has just come by and clinked glasses with me over the toast "*Bonne fête!*" He pours more of the Prestige Bordeaux to each friend (I guess they are friends) who come by, he pours some for himself, clinks, they leave. He reminds me of my son Theo, and I realize how great Theo would be if he were in charge of running a restaurant. As soon as I came in, this waiter sized me up and quickly recommended the soup, the steak, and the wine. And he has kept a close eye on me the entire time without making me feel watched. Three soup spoons from the bottom of my bowl, he asked me how I wanted my steak cooked. "*Au point,*" he called through the curtain.

✌

I slept long and hard last night, making up for the very long trek to the top of Montmartre and for still being awake at four a.m. the night before. I returned to bed, however, after a little coffee and croissant. While I slept for the next three hours, I knew I was dreaming spectacularly. I tried to enumerate the dreams while still dreaming so as to be able to write them down. On waking, however, I forgot to write them down immediately. There were five distinct dreams, but I could only remember three later; then, while walking past a window display, I recalled a fourth. Here is what I remember:

First Dream

Somehow it turned out that a new employee, a manager at my company, had a sideline hobby where by viewing large square frames rapidly (almost like watching 35 mm film, but larger frames), he was creating a new theory of perception. I had seen only one frame somewhere else, but seeing the potential concept, I traced it to his garage where his laboratory was set up. He was running these frames that were color images of people's families. He explained his ideas. I was agreeing, but also maintaining the demeanor of an owner of the company where he worked. I was deeply intrigued by the film, the method, and the theory. His children came and went, and then his wife came out to meet me just at the point when I was lying down to observe the film in the special way you had to lie. She greeted me with deference, spoke to him briefly. He also was lying down, explaining everything very carefully. He started whispering in my ear, and I realized that, theory or not, I was still the owner of the company where he worked, and I asked to leave.

(The waiter says no decaf but he has brought me a *digestif,* which is potent. "Nothing But a Heartache" is playing on the soundtrack. Whose is that raw voice?)

Second Dream

This dream was related to the first one. I was leaving the new employee's home when I saw through the windows of the garage that fires were burning sky-high in the blocks beyond. There were sirens and alarms and bedlam. I was frantic to get to my block, to see whether my house was in danger. The fires were all encompassing.

(Now a French cover of "California Dreaming" is playing.)

Third Dream

My friend Lynn Whittaker showed up with Brad Pitt, her new love, and they couldn't stop making out. They were all over each other. I was thinking: Lynn? Brad Pitt? Later she drew me aside to confide that yes, it was going amazingly, and she was going to ride this all the way to whatever end was in store. I slapped her on the behind as she left, and said something like, "Go, girl!"

(The waiter has commented that I am a writer, that he admires the ability, the spirit, the opportunity to take in the world and renew it accordingly—all of this in French. I told him he also must be a writer, but he said, *"Non, non, j'aime bien, mais non,"* and then "*je vous dérange trop.*" He has now distracted me too much by being so nice.)

Fourth Dream

Forgotten. (The Beatles' "Penny Lane" has just started playing.)

Fifth Dream

Someone had handed me back a manuscript that I had submitted for a competition along with a number of very distinguished writers. Along with my manuscript are others, and each has Doc Hall's initials and a note. On mine the note says, "With a little rewriting I'll publish this."

December 25, 2005
Sunday, 2:30 p.m., at Tea Time, in front of Centre Pompidou

Chai tea is delivered very quickly. It's nearly five dollars for a tea bag, milk, and hot water, but it's worth it at the moment. Though I have only been walking for an hour, I find my legs are just sick and tired of it. It's not good. The other pleasures of walking are too compelling, so the legs must just get over it.

(Now the soundtrack is African drums and a trumpet. Merry Christmas.)

Here is a brief summary of my Christmas morning in Paris:

8:45	wake up
9:00	croissants & coffee & yogurt
9:30	back to bed
11:00	read book on Shakespeare
12:30	bath
1:30	leave hotel, head toward Notre Dame

I walked through the cathedral among masses and masses of people under the concussive pressure of an organ played by, it seemed, a wild animal. After fifteen minutes of that, the whole "congregation" applauded. There were signs directing the throngs to *messes*, but no one within the cordons was praying. They were taking pictures just like the *visiteurs*. I abandoned the idea of being at a church service; there were no real signs, divine or otherwise, suggesting that I should stay. I did take one picture, at least, of the red insides of the stained glass windows.

With that particular activity dispensed with, I moved on, thinking to walk in different directions, but only made it one large block and came back to Notre Dame via the garden gates behind it. So, going on in what I thought to be another new direction, I realized (aha!) that I was in the same block explored yesterday, just from a different access. I was in *L' Hôtel de Ville*, a place where many were hanged in ages past. It currently features a huge igloo constructed to sell tickets to ice skaters for the rink beyond. Today, I found the expanse was full of toddlers pushing ingenious devices that kept them upright. Past the skaters, I found the outline of Centre Pompidou, which drew me to Tea Time. This catches us up to the minute. My last Splenda is now going into the last cup from this pot.

My thumb-joint problem wins out over the Maxilase. I will continue to take them anyway—little orange pills.

By virtue of walking the same neighborhoods day after day, I have access to a continual stream of people. What delights and encourages me the most are seeing the elderly couples: bundled against the cold, arm in arm, barely able to walk, yet walking, walking, walking. The lady of the couple almost always has dyed hair. She wears a beret of red, purple, or fur with a perfectly coordinated shawl or scarf. She usually also wears makeup, though not necessarily. I often see older women who wear no mascara, but have small, blue eyes—bright, almost glittering. I hope their serenity is not imagined on my part. I see others, as well, men and women alone, crippled, using a cane, the women are very stooped, but still making their way. They pass by as normal, a typical and essential part of life. At home, it seems, the elderly do not get the same opportunities to venture out and live.

As I walk on the streets here, I encounter crowds that seem so out-of-place that I feel local by comparison. They are mostly Asian students, but also streams of world tourists: Russian, Australian, American, even French. I see them with heads bent over maps that take two people to absorb. They're on a schedule; they need their photos taken right now in front of Notre Dame but pass over Centre Pompidou. Then they need a picture in front of the Seine, the place des Invalides, the Arc de Triomphe, but not St. Eustache. After a few days, I can now detect the accented French of the Arabs and Israelis, and the Germans (always easy) and the British. I can't hear my own accent, of course, but I wish I could.

Also, yesterday on Sebastopol, before I could take out my pocketed camera, a beautiful young man strode by in a focused and purposeful way, entirely dressed in the manner of the gentry from the mid 1700s. He wore a three-point, black felt hat, a blindingly white shirt with a frilly collar and sleeves, and a black, three-quarters coat fitted to perfection with double rows of gold buttons. I think he was also wearing white silk stockings, but he strode by too fast to be sure. While I couldn't see the boots, I'm convinced they were black as well. These garments looked like real, authentic goods. Not a costume. He strode down the street as if everyone else were dressed from the same era; he didn't even acknowledge the rest of the street staring in amazement. I never so regretted missing a photo, even including the ones denied me by Miss Chatty on the Ferris wheel.

❧

Two nights ago I did turn on the television in search of news, an old addiction that is, apparently, not entirely dead. There was only one business channel, however, in English. Then, last night, I watched the French edition of "Who Wants to Be a Millionaire?," which has a host who is much cooler than Regis. It's a good thing they printed the questions on screen because it allowed me to follow along. In fact, I would have won six-thousand euros. Ease must be key to the success of these shows—the idea that I, or almost anyone, could perhaps become so rich on this show. One of the questions was: "Why do American Indians dance?" The contestant wasn't sure, but she guessed correctly: to make rain.

I've been here an hour and no one is hassling me to leave. I am the only one in this plastic-enclosed-sidewalk-café portion of Tea Time. You enter through a slit in the plastic, a sort of door. I'll take a picture. I've now ordered a second pot because the waiter says that while they don't have Splenda, they do have an alternative to sugar. This is a great way to spend Christmas. The two pots of tea are expensive, of course, but look at the package they're wrapped in.

One of the young waitresses dances to the African drum music in the background. It's a bit incongruous. She is very white and blonde. Something makes me doubt she'll ever see Africa.

Surveying the street from here I can see other combinations of people, besides the usual couples. There are women of all ages, friends, walking arm in arm. Many wear unattractive overcoats: the quilted ones that make it look as though they're about to be shipped FedEx. I love to see the style young Parisian women adopt, however. Knee-high pink leather boots, not baby pink, but a shadowy pink, with the leather at the ankles a bit baggy and bunched up.

One thing you can absolutely count on: all females, including toddlers and grandmas, will be wearing scarves and wearing them artfully. One of my real, reckless pleasures has been to buy an assortment of the very thin, patterned silk scarves and wear a new one each day. My intent was to give them as gifts, but is that done? Can you give someone a scarf that you've been wearing? No? Then I'll have to buy a lot more. They're truly a bargain at five euros.

Something I don't recall from previous visits is a sweet bakery item called a *gaufre*—a Belgian waffle you can have with or without powdered sugar. They're everywhere, on corners and in restaurants.

℘

I have a recurring thought that someone I have known in my life, but have forgotten about, calls out my name, say in front of Notre Dame, just as I am about to return to rue Monge, which is by now a beaten path for me. At times it's Nelson (my third husband), temporarily separated in the crowd from Holly (his wife).

It occurs to me that this is what psychotherapy is all about: creating conditions for one's memory to come gradually to the top. This must be so that a riff might occur in a way that fills in some psychic hole. There are old flames, of course, but also friends from high school. Actually, I think more about the people from that era than from any other. For me, after all, high school years (1960-1964) were both the most formative and, in some ways, the most alarming.

A friend of mine married my first real sweetheart, after stealing my best friend. I want to tell her that, try as she might to put me out of her mind (as if she were innocent), no one is fooled, least of all me.

When I saw her and my sweetheart again, at the August 2003 reunion, I was truly struck dumb that a relationship formed in high school could really and truly last a lifetime, military and diplomatic reassignments notwithstanding. The survival of their marriage felt like a continuation of their regular showing up of others from those years at Dreux, my high school. Had I just tried harder, was the subtle message, I might be here with him today, actually hearing him call my name.

I could tell he was keenly interested in how I'd turned out (and so was she, of course). He and I were the only Ph.D.'s in the whole crowd of 200 from all four grades of our high school. She, meanwhile, had become a nurse. She kept the same exact figure she had then and had clearly begun dyeing her hair. She appeared youthful. He went baldish and gray, but in a very distinguished way.

I was dying to see him and wanted to remind him of the letter he wrote me after I moved to Germany, the one he signed: "Love always." (I wrote to Hansell [my elderly literary friend] about that letter.) The letter was about the sadness he felt over my moving and how only that, my moving away, could break us up. I wanted to tell him that the letter, with its closing phrase, got me through a very painful time during a divorce. A third divorce. At the time my first real sweetheart was one person I wished would just show up in my life again, if only so I could tell him about the letter and how friendly it felt to rediscover it in old, stored files just at the right time. It was consoling to read someone would always love me, even if written by a seventeen-year-old already dating the woman he would marry.

⅓

I have now spent two hours in Centre Pompidou, and I am very happy to have decided to go on in. I debated. I was drawn to the huge open space in front of this amazing structure—the architecture features pipes and exposed wires, conduit, tubing. It is so utterly unlike anything else in Paris. Even the Eiffel Tower looks like an old maid among old maids in comparison. At the time, I had been thinking about how much I would like to go in before leaving Paris.

What finally attracted me was a crowd that had gathered around a street performer whose French I understood with ease. I was disappointed that he occasionally stopped to translate into English—too bad for the Russians, Chinese, and Latvians. He was juggling three torches and riding a sky-high unicycle while keeping up a very witty patter that made us all roar with laughter. It is amazing how forms of art create such instant communities. All we had in common was anticipating his next *bon mot*.

From there, I felt motivated to go into the Centre where I saw a fabulous, mind-bending exhibit called "The Big Bang." The curators had taken all of modern art up through the late 20th century, irrespective of chronology, and classified the *oeuvres* by:

- The Body Comes Apart; the body takes a disarticulated form.

- Space Comes Apart; lines and shapes separate.

- Sex Comes Apart (including a bride sculpture by Niki Someone who died in 2002. What a phenomenal piece.)

- War Is Everywhere.

(There may be other categories—I'll check the "manifesto" later.)

The works selected did just what you go to a gallery for: open the mind, rearrange the mind, challenge and terrify, amuse, calm, and agitate.

I watched one flat screen for at least fifteen minutes while a video unfolded the days of the week represented by the artist entering a room with a bucket of paint a different color each day (Wednesday: orange, Thursday: green, Friday: blue). He takes a different approach to painting the room each day. On Wednesday, the film runs backward and the room is unpainted by the end of the "day." On Thursday, he paints the four walls and the floor deep, bright green. On Friday, the opposite wall from the door is first to be painted. This all occurs in record time. I would have watched it all, but I decided that was not required.

There was also a dark alley. Then a nonstop video of an arts-museum tour in which a really snobby lady in a suit and heels gives a tour, slamming all the artworks as drivel, then stopping at the water fountain or an exit door to rave on about how brilliant these works are, how transcendent, rare, inventive. "Substantial," she said of the water fountain. Hilarious.

There were so many amazing (how many times have I used that word?) artworks, some exploding out of the wall or from the floor. Every piece appeared well-chosen to create a balance between giving the viewer the upper hand and taking it away. I may go back just to make a descriptive list in hopes of just recreating the feelings and thoughts of visiting that exhibit.

At the end of the exhibit, it was very dark. I went to find the escalator down, but couldn't. On the way to the elevator, however, I looked out and was astonished by the view of the Eiffel Tower. Since being here, I've seen it lit up at night several times, but tonight (perhaps for Christmas) it was lit differently, in brilliant shades of white and golden lights. It shimmered with pinpoints of light like real diamonds matched on a watchband. I tried to take a picture of it, but it was impossible to capture. There are so many forms of art here. Paris seems only about art and the celebration of sex and war. It's as if the Big Bang all happened here; to some extent it did.

I come back by Notre Dame to Salon des Tartes and order *la jardinière*, allowing myself *fromage avec banane, chocolat,* and *dècaf* for dessert. I'd promised promised *promised* myself I would not consume another confection until walking back up to Sacré-Cœur and back. Oh, well.

I also reached my son Brandon, my sister Pam, and Mom today.

December 26, 2005
Bergamote

Dream

There's a huge house with many wings where I'm visiting a prosperous family. I seem to know the man and his wife as well as the housekeeper, whom I've agreed to help out because she's overwhelmed with tasks. In doing so, I get distracted and catch myself behind with work. I worry about disappointing the housekeeper. I begin to hurry up and cast about looking for things to do and tools to do them with. I open a door that turns out to be the couple's bedroom. Though it is late, the man is only just arising, coming around the corner naked. Neither of us is embarrassed, but I say something like, "Oh, pardon me." (I say this phrase daily on my walks when I bump into someone.) The man also resembles a nude figure I've seen in the museum of modern art. He is old, has gray hair, is wrinkled all the way down to his toes, but he has charm and dignity. He waves me on.

Later his younger wife all dressed in red—red winter coat, red knitted hat—cheerfully greets me on her way out the door.

The main revelation of the dream was that the house was the same one I've dreamt of many times. In my dreams, no matter how many wings you go into, there is one ultimate room of the house which is grandly furnished but sealed off, or at least generally unused. I always regret not being able to afford the house in my dreams, but resign myself to knowing that they, whoever they are, own it now. I wonder each time I have the dream if I'll finally be able to visit the room.

❧

I'm at Bergamote again, at last. Carrot soup and the white wine were divine, as expected. Unfortunately, the chicken casserole was not. I can't remember what the menu described as the unique herbs, but I couldn't detect any at all. I am not discouraged, however, and will certainly come back to try the herbed red wine, if nothing else. As I had suspected, you can't buy the wine bottled. I imagine that they have an infusion process here on site whereby a fresh herb is used to flavor the wine daily.

I have a decaf. I love how they serve the milk heated, in a little white pitcher. It's cold and blustery today, perfect conditions to try wearing my purple beret, but unfortunately this did not occur to me when I was dressing.

❧

Let me take a moment to record what I love about my room and bath: The room is tiny, so nothing can get lost. The head of the bed is less than two feet from the window (nearly floor to ceiling), and I can take in the cold fresh air. Of course, the street noise at night prevents overly long, deep sleep, but I still love the windows. The bed also has wonderful, fluffy pillows: two rectangular and two large square ones—perfect for the long hours of reading. It's a double bed with a wall lamp on either side. The light switches, for the wall lamps and the room lights, are easily reached. There is a little cabinet on each side of the bed—one side I use for apples and clementines, the other holds the phone.

The chifforobe holds the few items I need to hang up, plus it has a shelf for clean clothes, a shelf for laundry, a shelf for the turtlenecks. The bathroom has a long, deep tub with a hand-held shower device to rinse my hair. The sink has a swan-neck spout that makes it easy to fill and refill a plastic bottle; it also swivels 360° if you want it out of the way to wash unmentionables. The radiators, one in the room and one in the bath, are adjustable, so I was able to practically turn them off. It is a true pleasure to return to find the room all straightened with the top layers just folded down, as the housekeeping lady has noticed suits me better. One negative is that the mattress is indeed hard. I wake up with a backache every day, but that is what a very hot bubble bath is for: one in the morning for the backache and one in the evening to appease my legs after miles of walking.

How many miles will I walk today? I need to increase the number because the daily croissants are adding up. I wonder if this joint pain only begins to show what the next years will feel like—constant pain that doesn't prevent, say, writing, but never leaves consciousness.

৻৵

I had an unexpected conversation with Brandon on Christmas. He didn't have to work. We talked a really long time, and he sounded a little stuttery regarding a third attempt his company has made to bring him into management. He would have to go to full days, and he doesn't want to do that while Bailey is so young. Those kids have a truly fabulous dad; both of my married children are superior parents in the ways that count. I know that only too well.

❦

Having not read as long this morning after the bath, I am out and done with (this fairly excellent) lunch, and it's only two in the afternoon. I may try to go back up to Montmartre, as the exceptional feat of getting up there is what I've been most pleased with accomplishing so far. I could even see Sacré-Cœur for longer, now there's still so much daylight. We'll see.

December 27, 2005
On a chartered bus to Chartres. Nearly 2:30 p.m.

It actually snowed in Paris, and now the countryside is white, though the sun is also out and melting it fast. It was a bit of a thrill to be walking through snow to the Cityrama office to book this tour. The effect was very thick and lovely, though not sticking—just falling on your hair and into your eyes.

Earlier I had a clue as to what my accent sounds like—Italian. When I ordered a sandwich with *jambon* and *gruyère avec cruditès*, the guy working in the bakery said, as I left the shop on the way to Cityrama, "*buon giorno.*"

⁓

It is hard to do something so seemingly trivial and vain as write in a journal after seeing the cathedral in Chartres. To say that it's humbling does not begin to describe the effect. The experience of entering Chartres seems somehow more profound than seeing Notre Dame or any of the other cathedrals. The others become mere chapels by comparison. The guide informed us that fifty artisans probably worked around the clock for decades to shape the crude stone. The result is an endless series of statues, columns, and windows, no two patterns exactly alike, articulating the entire Bible for the illiterate masses. For example, there was St. Michael directing the damned to hell and the rest to heaven. The stories are told in stone and even more brilliantly in stained glass deeply infused with the cobalt of the 1100s. I try to imagine not only the process of making the glass blue, but also how to choose all the colors and make the design. How do you decide what to put into such a work and what to leave out? Then comes the actual, on-site assembly: first the medallions, each containing a narrative image, then the towering window itself, with chapter one at the bottom and chapter twelve at the top.

The day is bitter, icy cold. The guide dismissed all seven of us after a commentary on the history of this most wondrous human accomplishment, and I have had free time to walk around. The cathedral is on a high knoll and the winds are fierce (hence some additional flying buttresses). It's my bad luck to have chosen not to wear my ankle-length overcoat today. The panorama of the landscape is unexpected, so unlike Montmartre. Below, every structure has a distinct shape and color. The buildings are spacious, plain, and geometric. This is certainly not the dirty-lace horizon of Paris. I don't mean to characterize Paris as unsightly from afar, but it is a contrast. Eventually, the wandering led me to a *salon de thé*. It offered a great alternative to the winter bite outside, and I can't afford to buy stained glass anyway, nor replicas of tapestries.

So now I am in the loveliest *salon de thé* yet—Moroccan, with seating for no more than twenty on a crowded day, decorated in white and a pale green. Six of the seats are sofas with quilted white and green patterns. Two circular tables bear mosaic tiles. All of the furnishings, including the sofas, have wrought iron frames, which include little folding walls of iron curlicues about four feet tall to create, if one wanted, a space apart. The proprietress attends and helps me with the words for sweets I can't myself name—she selects three small ones, honey, phyllo, nuts and spice. The tea is just like that from Desert Rose: mint and honey, served out of a silver pot into a small gold-trimmed glass.

I place the hot tea glass against my aching joints. I try to imagine recreating this in Georgia, but nothing works. A silver teapot on a nearby shelf, however, does bring to mind the Moroccan student Nelson taught, who brought him a nearly identical pot as a Christmas gift one year. I believe it is still in my office downtown, in a window.

In fifteen minutes I have to find the bus back to Paris. Another perfect day, or more perfect, really. I wish I could find the words to articulate the visions I feel, walking across the original stones that have been smoothed and whitened by millions of footsteps distracted by pure awe. As I looked at those windows, I kept hearing the voice of the poet who tells the story of coming to Chartres in the company of another famous poet and the sudden, overwhelming sensation of seeing the color. Who was that poet? Was he reading someone else's story about two others, and were they artists or actors rather than writers? The bursting language makes me think someone was a painter. I recall the voice of the storytelling and its timbre and pace perfectly, but the actual details are lost for now.

❧

I was three and a half minutes late to the bus and the last to arrive. It took two full hours to get back to the center of the city. Who could not, on seeing blue ambulance lights threading their way through the miles of traffic jam, think of Diana's crash?

I am at Salon des Tartes for the fourth or fifth time now, and I went ahead with a twelve-euro menu. Walking here from Cityrama tours was treacherous in the extreme. All was dark, and the streets were coated in an inch of ice. That I know my way with ease was some help, as were the still-lit towers of Notre Dame.

In fact, it is not the fourth or fifth time:

Salade végétarienne – twice	2
Salade parisienne – once	1
La jardinière – once	1
Salade quatre fromages – once	1
Menu 12 € – tonight	1
	6

I have been here six times. This will not be my last either. I could hardly finish the four *fromages*, I recall. In fact, I left a great deal of shredded cheddar on the plate. That's one of the attractions— full value. Tonight the first course was a small salad with three (heads intact! gasp!) shrimp with avocado and grapefruit wedges. It was delicious. Now, there's a plate full of green beans and cur- ried squid. It's superb. It also comes with all the French bread you can eat, of course. The soundtrack seems somehow appropri- ate to the setting, although I am not sure why—"Listen to your heart . . . before you tell him goodbye." Earlier the same song played, and the waiter, a Chinese youth and the son of whoever owns this restaurant, hummed along. We're practically friends.

I am surprised by the kindness that the family who owns Salon des Tartes has shown me today. The restaurant cleared out early, and the youth left, waving "bye bye." The man he calls "Pa" came out and explained that I am welcome to stay and write. In fact, he brought me a decaf at no charge, then ten minutes later his daughter or wife brought me a huge, cold tangerine with a made- moiselle sticker. (How lovely and unexpected. Either my exces- sive writing—perhaps it creates an air of artistry? or of their being written up for a gourmet magazine?—or my repeated coming in about this time—cold, tired, and starving—has earned me these flavorful gifts.) I realize that the restaurant is now closed and that the crowd in back is actually a family reunion. How long does one stay pretending to write great literature so as to show proper appreciation for free coffee and citrus? I am tired, it's nine p.m., and I want to call Theo before I've fallen out of love with this day completely due to desire for sleep. Maybe I'll stay a few more minutes.

December 28, 2005
Salon des Tartes

[*Next to the beginning of this entry is placed a label*—Mousse de Mimosa *bath & shower gel—with this note:* "My bubble bath; I even had to buy a second bottle."]

I'm in Fontainebleau, just after touring the château where all of the kings of France lived, even if, as with Napoleon, only for a few months. I could not believe I was casting my very own eyes on the rooms where he studied and worked, sleeping at most two or three hours at a time, or so the guide said. From here he said farewell to his armies, signed his first abdication (April 1814) and then on to Elba. But his armies brought him back. I can't help wondering, having seen the Fontainebleau château, what Napoleon would have thought of one-way streets. I am emboldened to try to figure out how to get myself to Malmaison. The guide says it's just a train ride and a bus ride away.

It's snowing again. The sky is white, and there's a serious chill in the air. The next stop is Barbizon, an artists' colony. This time, I'm sitting behind the driver, perched on the most amazing seat in the bus. In front of me is a virtual IMAX, except we are actually riding into the screen. The windshield is that deep, that wide, and that immediately in front of me. I had to do queue battle to get this seat. It's worth it. On the way back I see a highway sign announcing Ris-Orangis—Derrida's neighborhood.

I saved a small sticker with a white background and a pink heart declaring "Pink Lady." This sticker is from the sweetest, most succulent apple you can imagine, purchased from a grocery shop on the main cobblestone avenue in Barbizon, birthplace of impressionism. Théodore Rousseau and Jean-François Millet left Paris to seek an alternative art form, one different from religious, historic, or portraiture painting. They studied nature in the second largest forest in France, shared by the royal hunters back in the day. Trees, cows, etc.

ℰℛ

Back to Salon des Tartes. Tonight I'm having *petits toasts avec* something, something *oeuf cassoulet de poulets,* and *haricots verts*—also known as "The Menu 12"—which is a great value. The something *oeuf* turns out to be an egg salad paste squirted onto little toasted rounds. They are delicious, healthy, and plentiful. (The background music sounds Italian.)

My exploration of Paris extends a little more everyday. I know, for example, that in my neighborhood, but in the opposite direction from Notre Dame, is the Gobelin tapestry factory. There they still make the same palatial-sized patterns that they did for the French kings' comfort centuries ago. Using the same methods, it takes seven years to complete a tapestry so large. I know that I can easily visit to watch how it's done. Or if that doesn't appeal, I can always go to the Museum of the History of Evolution (note: there's no confusion in France on this subject), or return to Montmartre to see Derrida's grave (and others'). I am officially writing off the Louvre. D'Orsay is still a maybe. Picasso is also a maybe.

Yesterday I glimpsed inside the Compound of the Mosque ("for the Musselman") and started up the maze cultivated around a sort of hill—do they call them hillocks?—at Jardin des Plantes, a major botanical garden and small alpine forest. The garden was quite a majestic little thing: dark, green to black, fresh and un-Parisian. I saw a cedar of Lebanon, 400 years old and grown from a seed planted by a priest, or was it a seed given to a royal person by a priest? Anyway, it appeared to be a lucky, healthy tree.

Each day more emerges to pull me into new ventures—therefore I haven't even written the first word of the article I'm supposed to be working on. Which reminds me of my dream last night. It was of Doc again, this time talking to me fairly intensively, and I am pretty sure it was about writing, getting started, and about his own book. Besides not working on the article, I've not been "shopping-shopping" even once. The boots and shoes were kind of an accident.

December 29, 2005
On a bus; Malmaison

Today, I made two major, quantum leaps (technically, one is only half leapt at the moment): I got on the Metro, and I got myself, without a guide, to Malmaison, Joséphine's home. You'd think it would be mostly about Joséphine, but really it's still about him. You find his toothbrush, his compass, his little pocket book on conducting war. Anyway, the traces of her were inspiring. Perhaps there was more of her, or of them as a couple, there than I give credit for. There was, for example, a whole room painted in those green stripes that they seem to have invented.

Now the reason I only say half leapt: I got myself out of Paris, but I haven't gotten back yet. It's only two-thirty, so I have about three hours before dark. I'm now at a tavern next door to Le Paniland Joséphine, taking a rest to settle my nerves. I'm willfully ignoring the part of myself that wants to contemplate how scarily far I am from rue Monge at the moment. I have ordered a decaf and a *paradiso*, some sorbet with sauce. The sorbets are labeled lemon, mango, and apricot and are drizzled with caramel. Contemplating espresso and gourmet dessert, there is only one correct response: *miam miam* ("yum yum"). There's also water, and a restroom. In fact, there are many practical reasons for taking this break, but mostly I'm just feeling thrilled to be where the Bonapartes contemplated their next steps. I bought a huge biography, *Napoleon and Josephine*, in the gift shop. I'm re-inspired to know this history in detail.

On the long walk here (the stranger in the Metro told me it would take forty-five minutes, but it only took thirty), I stopped in a grocery store and bought this cool pen, since the others are running out of ink. I got one for Steve (my business partner), too, not realizing they were fine point. It's just a Bic, but a French Bic from Rueil.

එ

It is still daylight as I ride the train (rapid transit) to Paris. It's snowing again.

එ

Fluffy snowflake clusters fell all the way to Albert I, the boulevard back at the train station. Every retraced landmark was like a touchdown that no one thought the B player could make. At that same France Prix, I stopped and bought twenty dollars worth of pens to celebrate. I am still not back to my hotel, but I am thinking of keeping my Ph.D.

December 30, 2005
Friday night Salon des Tartes encore

There are many reasons why I like Salon des Tartes enough to make it my nightly supper destination. It is non-smoking. There is delicious food, all over the map: squid, curry, spaghetti, huge salads, and each is imaginatively conceived. The soundtrack is pleasing and not too loud. Above all, the service is lovely and patient. The Chinese family who runs the place is a team: several or at least two are siblings with their spouses and children, and I think I have also seen aunts and grandparents. They shout the orders in Chinese down a little flight of stairs. The chef even poked his head up once. I have decided French in a Chinese accent is lovely and calming. They don't groan when they see me come in every night. The young man who waits on me sings the lyrics of all the songs regardless of language, just under his breath. He's so young, and I often see him reading a book in Chinese at slow times.

Today has been the only real bad luck day, and all told it wasn't so very bad. The worst was that the beautiful snow turned to rain mid-afternoon. As I no longer fear the Metro after yesterday's adventures, I actually rode it again. Unfortunately, so did everyone else in Paris, and the experience was one of drowning in a refrigerated stew of humanity. I disembarked. In the end, I just got back on after half an hour and returned to the hotel to begin reading the fabulous story of Napoleon and Josephine. It seems riveting enough to read on a rainy day in Paris.

Just before going in, though, I wanted to replenish the fruit, and thought I'd seen a little grocery store earlier just across the street. I ducked in quickly out of the rain, anticipating those sweet grapes and apples, but did not see fruit anywhere. The clerk said *au fond du magasin*, and so I went to the back. There were no grapes, only some rough-looking apples, not pink ladies. So, I got three apples, paid, and left to discover that right next door was the real grocery store. It was as if a 7-11, or some other soulless convenience store, had opened up next to a cute, Parisian version of Kroger. Here were the multiple check-out lines and the bustle of a larger store. I found beautiful fruit, including grapes, and bought a huge bunch of the sweet, white kind. It was only after I got back onto the cold, grey street that it hit me: hey, they had Diet Coke. A small, but persistent, part of me wanted to turn back.

Of the four destinations I tried to visit today, one was disappointing, one was just closed, and the last—Grand Lafayette—was simply too huge and crowded to deal with once I got there. At least one, however, was spectacular. Now this brings us to the good luck part of the day:

Spectacular

The crypt beneath the square in front of Notre Dame re-opened on the twenty-seventh, and I'm glad I remembered to come by again and check. Through the crypt, the most incredible ancient Roman ruins are revealed, owing to some excavations late last century.

The exhibit created around it begins with the very earliest Gauls who settled in the island in the Seine, calling it "Parisii." Owing to the exhibit, I now know that was 300 years BC. History brought the Romans, the Normans, the Germans, each leaving their cultural designs on the same bit of rock. It was quite amazing. They had several panoramas of Paris when it was only a river cutting across land sunken among buttes. In the panorama, I could see the one butte in particular which I am determined to climb again and pay my respects to Derrida—Montmartre.

Disappointing

While historical depictions of a place like Paris usually leave me spellbound, I was completely discouraged by the natural history museum. It was probably the swarms of children. (I only seem to like my own grandchildren when it comes to child appreciation.) There were some interesting marine dinosaurs on display, but the Noah's Ark of African-plains mammals containing wall after wall of winged and furry creatures—just added up to a huge bore. I was struck by a movie depicting natural history in Darwinian fashion looping on a large screen. The film starts with thunder and lightening over great waters, yielding amoebae, then jellyfish, and eventually a creature looking up from the depths at the sunlight, suggesting a desire to seek it out. Overall, it posed a stark contrast to our weird, national anxiety about history of this kind.

Closed

I made a huge effort to go to Gobelin Manufacture. I had wanted to see the tapestries made, the process using purportedly unchanged technology. While it was not open, I found a big French flag flying at the front of a Greek classic monumental façade decorated with scenes of making thread, dyes, patterns. It seemed a fitting front for a factory that makes beauty.

Overwhelming

The two previous visits to Gallerie Lafayette found me in all kinds of rapture at the Chanel counter and so on. Compelled to recreate the delectable sensations produced by colors of leather you've never seen before and shapes for purses you can't imagine, I boarded the Metro. The weather today, however, must have driven everyone to the same store at the same time on the same Metro. I just gave up. After buying a few gifts from the sidewalk vendors, I was out of there.

ళ

Cassoulêt de poulet is over, as is the wine and coffee. I return to room 52, Hotel Monge for a bubble bath and a late night of reading *Napoleon and Josephine.* Tonight I am very aware of being in the neighborhood where Gauls and Germans and Bonaparte himself actually walked. Or, in Napolean's case, rode a horse. This, after all, is where he was crowned emperor, at the very cathedral I have slipped by every day for two weeks to find my favorite restaurant, which, in an ironic twist, isn't strictly French.

December 31, 2005
Salon des Tartes

I'm at Salon des Tartes again. As all the times before were excellent, why not for New Year's as well? I ordered onion soup, a green salad, and a glass of Beaujolais nouveau. I know I ought to have ordered a more sensational meal, but, frankly, I'm down to the final euros, and I'm determined to make them last the next day and a half.

Today has been the most unique of all. I stayed in the room for the most part, reading my new book. Then I took a walk of perhaps a mile, ending at Bergamote for one last, wonderful meal there. This time I tried the herbed rosé. I'm sure you don't just sprinkle basil or rosemary into it; somehow or other the freshest version of the flavors come through. I can only guess at the method they use to infuse the wine, but I'm inclined to try at the earliest opportunity.

I saw a truck go by that claimed to be the best *deménagement*—and I loved the implication. I know, of course, that in French *deménagement* means "moving van," as in relocating a household. In the moment, however, I imagined it meant something like deconstruction, only applied to management.

ૡ

I've now written seventy of these little pages. Incredible! The reason I stayed in my room today was to see if I could, in fact, write an article on work-culture change. I was amazed and relieved to find four long pages (of a much larger notebook) fill up in less than an hour. I scared myself a little with my productivity, so I stopped. Why is it about giving over to a writing project that is so threatening it seems impossible? Looking back, the pages I managed (or, perhaps, *démanage*-d) are very suggestive of good text. My favorite line was something about a cyclonic force we call customers, or something to that effect. Deming and the demographers have truly created a monster.

January 1, 2006
Montmartre

I have awakened naturally about eight a.m. for the last week, and this, my last full day, was no exception. The sky, however, was unexpectedly dark, or more so than usual. It soon began raining heavily. I knew it would be out of the question to walk to Montmartre, so my plans changed to taking the Metro there. Then, however, I just stopped any planning altogether. This is my new skill: not to plan a project or consider alternatives. Just breathe. See what happens next. Sleep? Maybe. Read? Why not.

So I got back into bed after breakfast and a bath and read one thrilling episode after another from the life of Napoleon and Josephine: the revolution, the Directory, the Consulate, the *coup d'etat*. The storm continued, and I opened the curtains wider. Then it stopped, and the sun actually shone for a few minutes. Should I dress and head for the cemetery or read some more? Easy. So I read and read until every muscle was annoyed that there was no armchair for relief. This went on until after one p.m. The sun had disappeared by that point, but there was still no rain. So I dressed and studied the map one more time so as not to have to open it if the rain returned. The course took me by a Baccarat window, and if it hadn't been New Year's and a Sunday and thus closed, I definitely would have plunked down a hundred euros for a red glass piece. I was therefore, thankfully, protected from spending a lot of money today.

So onward to climb the butte, again. There was rue Blanche, and the Moulin Rouge, but I couldn't find the cemetery. I walked and walked and asked directions many times. I saw many of the streets of Montmartre. The sun finally came out, and gradually the air felt warmer. The long coat then became a burden on my shoulders, but my heart remained gladdened by the virtuousness of all the walking and the romance of the mission.

I was imagining a conversation with Derrida most of the way. In this imagined conversation, I was reminding him of who I was, and telling him about what I am doing now. When I met Derrida in Chicago, he wrote in my journal, including his address, since he'd requested I send him the photos I'd taken.

Eventually, it occurred to me that the train driver on the mini trains last week could have only been kidding when he listed Derrida among the dead in the Montmartre Cemetery. Everyone I asked seemed surprised that I was looking for him there. It made sense to me, however.

༄

I'm at Häagen-Dazs, another *salon de thé*. When I came in and read the expensive menu, I was surprised to see no *thé*. I was half way out the door when the guy behind the counter downstairs stopped me. I explained: "no tea on the menu."

He replied, "But we have the very best tea, *Mariage Frères*." He gave me a choice of tea bags, and there was even a decaf.

It's delicious, even if drunk out of a paper cup, sitting alone at a wooden bar and listening to MTV music played on the many flat-screen TVs upstairs. It's not a bad way to experience *Mariage Frères*. "*De voir ici l'abondance à la ronde mère des arts et des heureux travaux, nous apporter, de sa source féconde, et des besoins et des plaisirs nouveaux*"—this quote from Voltaire is written at eye level on a red wall encircling the little wooden bar. The gold letters are a foot high, in cursive. "When a Man Loves a Woman" is on the soundtrack now. I think the voice has fabulous passion in it. Listening to American music in Paris gives new depth and life to the songs. Even Napoleon would have hummed this song under his breath, I think. It has been fascinating to read long excerpts of his letters to Josephine. He sent letters at least daily, often three times a day, from whatever front he was currently at. Couriers left every few hours to send them.

The guy tells me that for some reason French people like to eat upstairs, and this place will be renovated "with a new concept" next year. He turns out to be the owner. He has another Häagen-Dazs store and wants to open one more. He tells me his name is Havib Khettou and is very unexpectedly friendly. The objective correlative (thank you, Ph.D.) would be Chick, or Steve; someone who can, if so inclined and if sufficiently intrigued, give someone a lot of interested attention. Yes, I did live in North Africa and, yes, I was looking for the grave of Jacques Derrida. He was especially impressed when I told him Derrida sent me postcards from Algeria. Havib keeps an eye on me even while waiting on customers. Eventually he reveals that he is an Algerian, of Berber origin no less, and so is his young cousin. As we talk, the cousin is scraping a container of caramel empty and filling a crock-pot to heat it. He takes a taste at the end.

It's getting dark. Should I leave before it gets any later? It has been nice to talk to someone who is a greater talker; all I have to do is ask or answer a simple question, and he takes over from there. I can see that Havib really doesn't want me to go. I give him my websites and phone number along with a friend's number because he wants to connect with a publisher. I'm nearly out the door a second time when he calls my name and says that if I am looking for great places for dinner he has several he recommends. He then joins me on the sidewalk in order to give me directions, except he says they're for "next time, because they are all closed tonight." He also says go to the Bon Marché to see fresh foods from all over the world—too late. I told him I wished I'd stopped by earlier because I've needed good insider recommendations. It feels as if I'd made a reliable and friendly connection all by myself, someone I could call on in the future without feeling it would be an imposition. Additionally, there's no burden of having to carry the conversation.

I walked by one of the recommended places. Right next door to Häagen-Dazs was Restaurant de Ruc or Café Ruc. He said they have great cheeseburgers. I immediately ruled it out. No, no, he said, many celebrities go there. So I looked in the window on my way back to Notre Dame. Indeed, many celebrity-looking people were diving into plates of fries and burgers, all in a very elegant atmosphere of linen and china and crystal. I wonder if I saw anybody who was actually famous.

&

I'm now at Salon des Tartes for the last time. I was down to my last twenty-euro note when I stopped to get grapes and clementines. After my fruit purchase, I felt sure there would not be enough money to pay for supper, so I hurried to the nearest cash point for another twenty. This led me to buy an entire carafe, not just a glass, of Beaujolais nouveau, which is just the tastiest red wine. I told the young man who always waits on me that this would be my last night. A few minutes later, his sister brought me a plate of round crunchy things and a glass of champagne. I think she said "banana champagne." Is that possible? All I know is that this is truly New Year's and what I am holding in my hands is truly champagne and a gift at that, as was the cup of tea at Häagen-Dazs. I have more to say about that proprietor, but let me just say today has been just lovely, even though the cemetery was closed, and therefore no Derrida. Everything comes full circle on this trip as I sit in the same place that I did nearly two weeks ago. The generosity of the champagne is just amazing. No one else seems to have a glass, so I don't think it's automatically given. Wow, I have a carafe of wine as well as banana champagne. Happy New Year!

The curry beef tart is wonderful. There hasn't been a dish they've served me that hasn't been very satisfying. Not until tonight, however, did I completely understand that tarts-as-meals, not just for dessert, are their specialty. They are all made on the premises. A couple of days ago, I happened to be here when the fresh vegetables, along with every other provision, arrived at the door in a van. The whole family, including a boy who looked about my grandson Otto's age, formed a chain to hand off the boxes and bags and bottles, all talking together. The family feeling here is so incredible.

They have just come to my table and offered me more salad to go with my tart. How can I refuse? I am very touched by their recognition of my attachment to this restaurant, and by their showing me a similar attachment. The dialog has been entirely of gestures and expressions, since I don't speak Chinese at all and my French does not extend to "this is not a scallop, this is a shrimp." Here they call a shrimp a *gamba*, and a scallop a shrimp, which is fine unless you were really looking forward to *coquilles St. Jacques*, expecting white, spongy things.

ख़

There are no fewer than four James Dean impersonators in this Salon des Tartes restaurant on the first day of the new year. Nearby is a table of two young French women and three tourists. The French women are having an intense conversation, one with a pixie haircut sticking out everywhere, the other with delicate enameled butterfly earrings, the bottom half matching her orange shirt. The tourists are a group of one man with two women. Black binoculars lie on the table in front of them. The man constantly wipes his right eye with the mint-colored napkin.

Three long tables pushed together at the back are where members of the family that owns the restaurant sit. At present, only a young man and woman are sitting there. Perhaps they are cousins? The woman is really pushing it fashion-wise, with a baseball cap over her long straight hair, bejeweled extravagantly. She also wears skinny jeans and pointy-toed boots. Somehow I don't see her washing dishes here. (The soundtrack plays that song with the saxophones. What is that song? "And forget about everything. . . . He's a rolling stone. . . . You're going home." How exactly appropriate.)

I have a heated rhubarb tart, a half glass of the wine, and the whole glass of champagne left. This is one of those affirming moments, the kind that make you glad you didn't totally quit, give up, walk away, wash your hands of it, pull the proverbial trigger. Granted, it's still raining outside, so no lovely snow, but outside is also Notre Dame, and I'm in the exact place where Napoleon razed the houses on either side to make way for the coronation procession. In a wonderful understatement, the author of the book describes residents as "reticent." As a result of that coronation, however, we have so much. The Napoleonic code is still intact (with a few liberating changes related to women). We also have, in place of a few houses, long forgotten by now, this Salon des Tartes where a Chinese family shows unexpected hospitality to a total stranger on New Year's Day. Paris has so many ways of improvising beauty, maybe horrors as well, what do I know? I only know how long I wait for moments such as this.

One of the women tourists now rests on the shoulder of the man; his eye must be okay by now. He examines the dessert menu. The girl with the butterflies holds a cell phone to her ear and sings to her companion—"dee dee DEE dee dee DEE"—I guess she is imitating a busy signal. The man with the two women opens the dark chocolate that they serve with the coffee here. (From the speakers, Shankar's daughter sings from her first CD; my mind draws a blank on her name and the title of the CD. Nora? Laura? That velvet jazz. Sunrise, sunrise . . . Jones! Norah Jones.)

❧

My first wake-up call will be at six a.m. tomorrow. I have much to say about what this trip has become to me. I wish someone would pay me my current salary just to read, walk, sleep, dream, and write in a journal, occasionally in Paris. I have on this two-week vacation learned:

- To sleep as long as I want to, and to go back to bed as the first order of the day, near a window whose full light permits obsessive reading just before returning to clear, climactic, and important dreams.

- To totally ignore the time of day except to notice occasionally "oh, my, look at the time," without changing the pace of the activity.

- That I can walk literally for six hours non-stop.

- That I can write in a journal (despite the occasional excruciating pain) sufficiently in depth to remind myself that I was a writer once and could be again, even if I am the only reader and critic.

- That I can overcome the greater fears, which would otherwise close doors to really important experiences.

- That, while I enjoy modest luxury, I am well prepared for a poor life as long as I can enter a library on a regular basis, and take hot baths every day.

- That I can survive losing my jobs and house and car and many of the services that I currently subscribe to.

- That I deeply admire all three of my children for completely different reasons.

On that note, how is it that I have three amazing children? One thread they share that eluded me is a deep and daily attachment to their own family members and, in Theo's case, to his circle of friends on at least two continents.

☙

More versions of James Dean come in. There has been a bit of turnover. (And my handwriting has become looser.) I have become, predictably, slightly tipsy, and I want to finish this glass of champagne nonetheless. Since I am wealthy again with my twenty euros, I will need to drink some coffee. That six a.m. wake-up call is becoming a menace. I won't be allowed to sleep in any more for a long time.

One of the women, the one facing me, who had her head on the man's shoulder, stares at me. Why? I renew my lipstick and see that at most there are two sips of champagne remaining. Behind me is Notre Dame, to the right, an untried Japanese restaurant called Zenyama (what else?) with a small neon sign in red ("Restaurant Japonais") and purple ("Non Stop"). Something about that is too disconcerting—I realize I don't want to leave, yet I do want to get back into my bed and finish the grand history of Napoleon and Josephine. Earlier today, I left her before the divorce that she's been dreading for several chapters now. I want to take the ultimate bubble bath, eat some clementines, and pray for early sleep so as to mute the irritation of the wakeup call. I am already completely packed, the shuttle to Charles de Gaulle is confirmed, and my only worry now is whether I can get through customs and fully, fully reclaim the nearly twenty percent tax that I have paid to all regular vendors. The items from the *marchés* won't count because there was no paperwork exchanged.

Here go the two sips all at once. The two women have gone to the restroom while the man guards their jackets. The two young women are still chatting. And the family table has given way to two "howlies." That is what Hawaiian people call white people.

How do I know this? I am reading *Hotel Honolulu* by Theroux. On this trip, I have also finished his *Blinding Light* as well as Greenblatt's *Will in the World*. The latter is an absolutely fabulous explanation of Shakespeare's totally unrecorded life as extrapolated from his plays, from those of Marlowe and Kyd among others, from public records in Stratford, London, and English history of the time in general. Just a riveting read.

The two howlies drink Coke. The three look around to be sure they aren't forgetting anything, and now they leave. Goodbye. *Bonne Année.*

My joints, the right thumb most intensely, are killing me. I stopped the Maxilase yesterday evening to see whether it was really helping. Now I know why so many people are upset with Merck for having recalled their drugs. I need to make this pain a friend, for I plan to do a lot more writing by hand.

The family has allowed me to stay here now well over an hour without hovering. After the coffee, it's back down Lagrange to Monge, to the key at the desk, then to room fifty-two, haven for two weeks. Then I have scheduled: bath, book, sleep, dreams, alarm, bath, down the elevator, shuttle van, airport, home, and work, work, work.

January 2, 2006
Hotel Monge

I'm going home today! I now await the final coffee and croissant, with blackberry yogurt this time. Having gotten my luggage down, myself dressed (reverse order that), paid the bill, and come to breakfast all by 7:10 proves that I am still a heavy lifter despite these fifteen days of being on an infant's, or a cat's, schedule.

I dealt with a bit of emotion as I paid the bill. The emotion comes, I think, from a feeling that this may never happen again. Finishing *Napoleon and Josephine* was revelatory. I read deep into the night, determined to finish it while in Paris. I knew I probably wouldn't sleep well anyway and, in fact, was looking at my watch at 5:50. Imagine how surprising it was to get teary-eyed when Napoleon finally tells Josephine, who had been expecting it for years, that he needs a divorce "for France." It's truly emotional. The author, however, was not writing a potboiler. Throughout this massive book, she keeps a clear eye and style, reporting in a tone of observer and relying on quotations from their letters to one another as well as from letters and memoirs of all the many circles elbowing (and murdering) for power. All sources appear to mirror the passion the two express in their letters. It was an odd thing for Napoleon, so ruthless in every other way, to be completely captivated by Josephine through all their years together and even after her death. He went to the room at Malmaison where she died and was described by her daughter as full of tears when he got back to Paris. I was originally looking for a story about a woman whom I'd recalled as betrayed by something, her husband? Her country? The evil Bonaparte clan who hated her? What I found instead was a love story.

It was intellectually fascinating (or maybe just the vulgar thrill of an ambulance chaser) to have read this book feverishly over the last three days. I continue discovering within the story, even late last night, the names of the statesmen, courtiers, generals displayed as roads, all at those crazy angles on my now-crumbling map. Streets that I've been navigating since December eighteenth have not only been the sites of SS executions (the one historic event that escapes no one walking near the Seine). For example, here or there is the place where Louis XVI was guillotined and where Napoleon also celebrated something or other, perhaps his own coronation. The Tuileries gardens, Louvre, place de la Concorde, rue St. Honorée, and the Opera House all become vivid elements of the world Napoleon and Josephine presided over during the five years of the Empire. I'm especially captivated by the coronation at Notre Dame and, five years later, the second coronation at Notre Dame to underline Napoleon's status as emperor—an emperor, you see, being completely different from a king.

I learned this fine distinction along with many others: the Jacobins (extreme left wing), the constitutionalists, the ex-constitutionalists, the regicides (most extreme left wing), the *sans-culottes*, the royalists. All fall on a scale with the objects being to retain the Bourbons on the throne (that's the royalist side), to have peasant rule without religion (Jacobins in love with Rousseau and the exaltation of the primitive), or to install a royal-ish person along with a constitution (that's an emperor, or at least what Napoleon said to the gasping Consuls).

I returned to place Vendome and this time, instead of Chanel and Versace, I paid attention to the towering monument forged from the melted cannons of the enemy taken at Austerlitz.

I could go on, but read the book and visit Paris. The shuttle is nearly here.

2007 TRIP

December 21, 2007
2:30 p.m. Salon des Tartes (Again. At last.)

I have left my 2005 journal at home, deliberately. But so many contrasts and continuations are vivid even without that reference. In fact, now that I am back in Paris, the memory apart from word is stronger. Sometimes words just cannot distill all the layers of history and emotion.

Mme Julie is no longer at the hotel. What a huge disappointment. She was my only friend, to whom I brought tulips on Christmas Eve twice, and had hoped to again this year. I have her address, though, and I will send a card instead.

Here's the best and most decadent part of being back in Paris. I took my first long bubble bath at the hotel. In my life, I truly believe there is no greater comfort—especially here, where the tub is so deliciously deep. I put what little gel I brought in my hair, combed my hair back with my fingers, and then went to bed with wet hair.

After a three-hour sleep, I awoke to the shouts and chasing sounds of very young children playing in the amphitheater nearby, which dates back to Roman BC time. When I got up, I found my hair had dried and set in a sort of pompadour. It was really a great look. I just brushed through it and stepped out onto a sunny street. I was out in the world of Paris, passing myself off as the real Sherrie Ford. In truth, however, I must have been real enough to anyone looking, including myself. So gray. So old. I am not complaining—today. Just seeing it from a new angle. There is always that certain, distinguished air that graying Parisians have.

Regardless, as soon as I left the hotel, I had the sensation of knowing where I was. I found that, absurdly, the little restaurant near the hotel still has that red neon sign: "FRENCH FOOD." I stopped in at the Rock hair salon, the place where Gwen got her really great haircut on my second visit here, to ask about hair gel. There was none. Next to that was the *pharmacie* and, yes, they had both hair gel and eye-makeup remover. I had my first brief conversation in French. I confirmed that *change* is also used to mean "change," as in coins after breaking a bill.

Then like a magnet, not even needing to read street signs, I felt myself drawn to Notre Dame. To my great relief, I noticed Salon des Tartes immediately. Assured that my anchor for food and friendly service remained secure, I pressed on. The scene on the street had the same overall character, but I noticed differences in a few particulars. The beggars this time, for example, weren't Bosnians carrying written cards to express their homelessness, but rather, at least in one case, a beautiful young boy on his knees, holding a cup with his good arm, the other arm exposed with bandages. He also seemed foreign, but I didn't get close enough to see the extent of his case. Everything always goes up a notch.

Still obeying this magnetic pull, I stopped just short of Notre Dame at a *tabac* to get large sepia post cards and stamps. I saw a lovely poster in the window and found the courage to ask for it. *Affiche* (feminine), I now know, is the word for poster. I hope to collect more on this trip. On the way, someone French asked me for directions. I love that. To be asked for directions in Paris makes me feel in place.

ℭ

I'm now back at Salon des Tartes. (Oh, joy, it's still here.) I've ordered the same thing that I first ordered the last trip: *salade végétarienne*. The young boy who waited on me the last trip has matured a lot in two years. He, of course, does not recognize me. It will be interesting to see if he will begin to remember me over the next two weeks. The father and a woman I think may be the oldest daughter, or perhaps the boy's mother, are also still here.

Salon des Tartes has changed its menu—added to it, actually. I note they have a rhubarb tart, and I predict having one of those before the new year. I can't help but note that a new age-y muzak tape with piano trills has replaced the soundtrack I so enjoyed as background to my writing last trip.

As I plot the adventures ahead, I realize I am too enamored of repeating all the favorite turns from two years ago. I need to let that go and try new things. Of course, I will keep Salon des Tartes, Notre Dame, and the hotel as my beacons, but, otherwise, I plan on taking new directions. We'll see. Time to pay the bill and go back—it's only half past three, but I am feeling very tired.

December 22, 2007
Salon des Tartes

Tarte Provençal: eggplant
Tarte Rhubarbe
Riesling and *decà crème*

This has been a splendid day. Where to begin? I awoke in time for *petit déjeuner* (which ends at ten o'clock) and a long, hot bubble bath. This year, my room has windows that face away from the street, so it's much quieter. The bathroom is *white*—electric white, glaring white. The ceiling-to-floor window also faces the mirror, which in turn reflects the white tiles around the bath. The bubbles are extra foamy in this water, rising to new heights. Picture all that white and only red fingernails for color. Imagine deep breaths as you sink down into the hot water. After the bath, I took a nap for several hours, filled with dreams. Or did the nap come first, then the bath?

Leaving the hotel for the day, I stopped at the desk and arranged for five daytrips next week. They should help to focus my Paris days, and indeed, a mere six hours later, I have checked off the few mini-ideas I brought with me: buy black shoes, get l'Occitane bubble bath, wander around the Tuileries, and find out if Musée de l'Orangerie was open again; it was, so I went inside.

It took me by surprise. Two years ago, an artist recommended the museum as he sketched my portrait. He suggested avoiding the Louvre even, as, he said, Musée de l'Orangerie was by far the best. Who could have known how exceptionally right he was?

I rented the audio tour, as I have learned it's worth it, and accepted instructions in French. I knew full well this would mean I would understand only some of what the woman on the recording said. What actually happened, until I could figure out the whole system, was that I pushed a number and heard the details of a masterpiece, but never the one in front of me: a Picasso description in front of a Cézanne and, later, the reverse. There I was, experiencing these incredible paintings through the auditory overlay of a different work. The described works so unlike yet also like what you're viewing, and all so different from what you would say about them.

It was so postmodern. I am thinking this is likely how postmodernism came about: experiencing an artwork (perhaps a text or sonata) while inexpertly trying to understand it using a flawed critical technique. The result is a different kind of aesthetic experience and knowledge. Perhaps it also leads to a superior order of rationalizing ineptitude, or simply vanity, in not wanting the instructions to be given in English. So many clashing codes: language, tapes, and commentary.

Once I finally aligned the tape and the art, I found it almost stranger to hear the commentary for the correct image. For example, I puzzled that the image in front of me should be of desolate women when they were barely sketched in at all. Being barely sketched doesn't mean desolate to me, but maybe unseen, un-seeable, mysterious, dreamy, or just sleepy. The experience called into question the validity of renting the tapes as a means of understanding the works.

In the end, I think the audio was a good thing. What caught my ear looking at the wrong picture (for example, "the fading color of the candles on the piano") became a goal to find in the right picture. I felt I was bringing to life some aesthetic theory akin to "reader response," the theory that gives most of the credit to the reader for drawing any sort of life, story, or image out of a work. The artist only begins the process.

(Here the much-anticipated rhubarb tart arrives. Mmm . . . so warm. With the addition of a sip of Riesling, it becomes a phenomenon.)

To return to writing about the museum experience after this delicious break, I saw wonderful Picassos and Cézannes. The main event, however, was the infinite experience of the Monet master-work *Water Lilies*: what phenomenal scale and what a compelling story. A man in his last years found the strength and genius to escape the easel and paint on a scale such as Michelangelo, except instead of ceilings, he painted the height and length of two long, oval rooms flooded with natural light. Here the ceiling is a sort of white gauze that I guess must diffuse direct light.

At four p.m., I watched a long film about this masterwork, and I came out of Musée de l'Orangerie (yes, it was once an orange grove—for the palace Louvre), giddy with extreme visual delight-edness. The feeling came not only from what I'd seen on the curved and straight walls of the museum, but also from emerging to discover the scene outside. A full moon hung high and pearly in the twilight, the Ferris wheel was lighting up, and the sunset had just started to turn the feathery sort of clouds red and pink. I took a frenzy of first photos and left with the special satisfaction of capturing an experience that was both real and mine.

Here is a (completed) shopping list:

- Les Halles: I've bought eight scarves and shawls now, and there are still more to buy. Last time I could hardly find any, but this year, they're profuse—and of such better quality, color, and design, too.

- *Herald Tribune*: The price has gone up twenty cents. I was sad to read of the death of Arabella Spencer-Churchill.

- Gray felt boots with grippy, rubber soles: While black shoes are so French, I chose these boots because I have always felt I needed gray footwear.

What could make shopping difficult this year, however, are the color trends. Orange is the color for accessories, winter coats, and everything else. It's a persimmon orange, more yellow than pumpkin. It is not a color I envision taking home with me.

I have finally figured out the main difference between my current outfit and my triumphs and struggles with clothing from past trips. The black wool coat with the (fake) fur-trimmed hood keeps falling off my shoulders and hindering my full, fast-walking gait. It hits me; as with other shifts in garment fit, it is too large. I'm pleased to say a drastic increase in walking over the last two years has led to a pretty stable, smaller self. I start to think about finding a new winter coat here in Paris. After all, this one was either very inexpensive or on sale, so it would be no real sacrifice just to leave it behind. As I go further in this thinking, I wonder if I would have the nerve to buy a jacket like the one I saw on a young Asian woman earlier today. It was a brown, quilted coat, but with a sort of drawstring hem that caused the bottom half to act like a large bubble, pulling in at the calf, billowing out from the waist. So chic. The girl looked like a young Vera Wang. Her mother was also dressed in similar colors. I saw how carefully put together they were, with clean lines and neutral colors.

᷈

"*Decà crème*" was how my coffee order was turned in, and I confirmed with the waiter, "*Decà crème?*" He nodded. Now I know how to order properly. There are twin boys about eight years old here tonight. They are obviously part of the family, but I don't remember them from before. I envy their fluent French.

December 23, 2007
Bergamote

I have returned to the same lovely routine—sleeping till I wake, waking thankfully in time for *croissant* and *baguettes* with strawberry jam, then stowing the three little cheeses and remaining chunks of bread in my pocket for later. Both nights about midnight this has come in handy—I am still on Georgia time, but advanced one hour today.

I'm already checking on doors for signs of opening hours during the holidays. It's Sunday, and tomorrow is Christmas Eve, then Christmas. I am slightly concerned, as options narrow for the holidays. Last time, however, I had no problem finding open and delicious options.

I find that Starbucks in Paris does not take American gift cards.

Continuing down the checklist: I am back at Bergamote, and have ordered the *salade la Café Bergamote*, which contains shrimp, among other things. The restaurant is exactly the same as I remember it. The same young-Virginia-Woolf-just-tinier woman even greeted me. It turned out to be an accident, however, as this is not her table, and it is very busy here today.

The only person of color here is a toddler here with two larger, white American women. The child is a girl, her hair stands straight up about three inches, and she is dressed in a turquoise, velour hooded-outfit and tiny Nikes. She's well behaved as the women talk earnestly, then laugh. I notice they have very Midwestern accents. Next to me, about fifteen inches away (this is a small restaurant), sits a young American manager type, traveling alone today, with his computer bag occupying the other chair.

The herbed wine is wonderful. It's infused with basil this time. To me, this is the only place where wine truly tastes like a friend to the palate. This salad is absolutely huge—filled with salmon, shrimp, a whole avocado, and a variety of strong and mild greens (and purples, too). It was all covered with a delicate dressing that I left no drop of, using the bread to excellent final effect. I am smug in my ordering "*decà crème*" to the surprise and smile of the waitress. I may be an aging American on my own, but I (now) know how to order a coffee.

This day is so warm that I come out without the coat to slow me down. Now, where to today? I could climb to Montmartre. We'll see.

December 24, 2007
Chez les Filles

After leaving Bergomote yesterday, an extraordinary day unfolded. I had not intended to spend much time on St. Germain Boulevard. While walking back on the other side, however, I rediscovered some stalls set up especially for Christmas shopping. In the little market, wares from around the world, which are generally very colorful, are sold out of cheery, alpine-style stalls.

I was by then shivering from a slightly cooler day than expected. It turns out that leaving my windows wide-open for fresh air may not be the most accurate way to judge the actual outside temperature. Anyway, I was already primed to spend money on something before I reached the little stands. So, due to the temperature, instead of buying a chic, brown quilted affair as planned, I bought a knitted sweater-jacket from Ecuador. It has the brightest shades of orange, blue, purple, yellow, lime, and red. There's also some black (so black ski pants will still look okay) and a long, pointy hood.

I've had several compliments already. The first to compliment its beauty was the boy who sold me the jacket from the Ecuadorian stand. I took his picture. The most effusive, however, was from a nun in a candle shop run by a monastery—later in the day as I headed back to the hotel.

From the Ecuadorian stand, I went farther along, tempted by every display but losing all resistance at the Russian shop, which was selling Austrian crystal rings set in silver. Who knew that crystal could be so dazzling and brilliant, just the way that diamonds are. I bought three identical ones, one in orange, two in bluish-lavender, thinking of Beth and Donna. After my ring purchase, I walked back to the hotel to be certain my day trips had been arranged. They hadn't.

&

Fast forward to today. After wearing the orange ring all day yesterday, I returned directly (after a stop at the ATM) to the stand and bought six more. Who knows for whom? I feel very much the way Josephine had to have felt when she suddenly had more bounty than she possibly could fully own.

On the way to Les Pyramids, which is where you buy the day-trip tickets in person, I looked up to see a cinema poster for *I'm Not There*—the film not about Bob Dylan exactly, but about playing around with the idea of Bob Dylan in the world. It was a film I didn't think I would have a chance to see at home, unless it should come to Ciné, the local arts theater. Inquiring within, I learned that the next show would be at quarter to seven, plenty of time to retrace the way to Les Pyramids. Also plenty of time to find the post office to mail cards and even time to check whether Salon des Tartes would be open at half past nine (it wouldn't be, but I managed to get there by quarter past, just after the movie).

The experience of seeing a movie in this tiny theater was interesting. Looking back, I realize I misunderstood the queue process. I thought I was going to the end of the line but actually went to the front. So confusing. In the end, I got an excellent seat, in very close quarters with a hundred Parisians. I had this thought: here is a selection of people at least as interesting as any I could hope to meet. There are many of us with gray hair (we are really the only ones deserving to call the shots on this occasion). There were, however, also many young people, including two silly girls sitting to my right whom I inwardly threatened to smack for their shrill and endless chitchat through the interesting—if equally endless—ads and previews.

Finally, the movie played, and it was splendid. I was so glad it was in English, subtitled in French. The album for the soundtrack would be heavenly to hear on its own. I'm sure I heard Richie Havens in there. Anyway, the overall structure was similar to *Crash* and *Babel* in that it had multiple character-driven narratives, the best lines going to Cate Blanchett, though I personally loved watching Heath Ledger. The black actor playing one version of Dylan was the most impressive overall, Richard Gere the least, but then his story line was the oddest, and I'm sure I didn't follow all the heavy symbols.

After the movie came a rushed walk to Salon des Tartes by moonlight. The full moon was huge and slightly blurred around the edges. It appeared creamy, gentle, and somewhat lonely as the biggest thing in the sky.

I was just in time to ask the proprietor—the father surely, who by now remembers me from two years ago—what he would prefer that I order, given that they were about to close. He volunteered (again I'm speaking French and can only imagine what I'm actually saying and he is actually hearing) *tarte chèvre*. I know this means goat cheese. It was delicious, though my suspicious side suggested it may have been the un-ordered item all day long.

I was glad to see another regular was also there at that hour. I remembered the elderly man from last time. Everyone treated him with affection and he, in turn, must have said "bravo" a dozen times, referring to his supper.

So, having had the presence of mind to buy four tangerines

and one apple earlier, I closed the day with an excited walk back to the hotel, knowing that fresh fruit would be better than a rhubarb tart (from one perspective) and that many books awaited a long, restless night stuck in another time zone.

⁊

Now onward to today: Monday, Christmas Eve, with the plan mainly to get money, buy more Austrian crystal rings, go to the restaurant Chez les Filles, and in general find what else Paris will reveal to me—all of this to complete when I begin at half past two in the afternoon.

In the meantime, a couple of memories have come back to me from the past couple days, and I want to jot them down while they are still recent.

A memory from two days ago: It was at night, and while making my way home in the crowd on one of the bridges crossing the Seine (not Pont Neuf), I came upon a man playing cool jazz on the saxophone. Suddenly, he switched to playing the theme from the "Flintstones" cartoon as a crowd of young siblings came strolling by. They did not toss any coins into his box.

Another memory of two days ago: I was in the old Halles on Rivoli near the Louvre (I admit that I bought souvenirs there, as well as Diet Cokes and a crepe), when I saw a card stand with cards containing historical facts for every day of the year. Of course I looked at the one for September seventh, and it told me, among other things, that Buddy Holly was born on this day in 1936.

Moving on, the thought went through my mind—as it often does, this thought—"Why are you always focused on yourself?

Your birthday?" So I went back and found the one for my daughter, Juniper, March sixth, and the card said that on this day in 1939 Buddy Holly was born. What an interesting coincidence to have the same celebrity born on both my and my daughter's birthdays.

☙

I am now at Chez les Filles. I found this place out of a book my sister Melanie gave me for Christmas. The address is sixty-four rue du Cherche Midi, a very interesting name for a street. The restaurant lives up to its description: modest, warm, and delicious. By the way, the napkins are orange.

The quarter carafe of white wine leaves me a tad affected, and the Berber china in front of me has not a grain of couscous remaining. The meal was called *Tagine du Jour* and was described so enthusiastically by the lady that I ordered it. The dish was some sort of meatball, while the rest was spiced vegetables, including tiny black peas, and all over a bed of real couscous, not the kind out of a box. Apparently, not everyone understands *decà crème*. This waitress prefers *déça au lait*.

Beautiful! My coffee is served in a white pitcher along with milk, heated, in another little white pitcher. I drink the last of my wine . . . and feel very sleepy. The hotel is miles from here. I've walked and walked and walked, pretending I am thin and slightly younger. It has been exhilarating to find that the young lady at the hotel was right—walking alone at these hours of the night is little different from the daytime. I am so brave. Frenchmen included, people continue to stop me and ask directions. I must exude universal savvy.

December 25, 2007
Le Relais Gascon, Montmartre

[*A card is pasted above the following words:* "I picked up this card picturing shawls. It has nothing to do with today, but only with this fetish I've acquired over the years for shawls. These were too expensive, but if I have euros left over I may go in there and spend some."]

It is Christmas at about half past three. The only plan was to try to get up earlier (I did), and out on the street earlier (I did not), then get a crêpe at St. Germaine where it crosses rue Monge (I did). I then went to Pompidou Center to see if they had spectacular pens to choose from, but the museum, unlike last time on Christmas, was closed.

The next goal was to make my way to Montmartre by a totally different route (I did, on Sebastopol, but regretted it). All of a sudden: the street was not cleaned, buildings were crumbling, and every other store was a run-down MGB, which apparently means Black Beauty Center. There were all these places with Afro King on the marquee.

The overall plan was to walk more than ever, just go over the top with walking, and the journey to Montmartre, regardless of route, will give you that. But I saw no salons on Sebastopol and there was no slowing down, though I did pause to look long at Gare de l'Est and Gare du Nord, two landmarks in the run-down area.

I've ordered French onion soup and French fries. I found this little pub just a few blocks from Moulin Rouge, and I can see the cemetery from here, the one I went on a quest for on New Year's Day 2005 and found locked. Mmm . . . French fries in France are heavenly. I asked for mayonnaise half way through the mountain of fries, and they brought me a full crème brûleè dish of it.

I read that Paris will soon be a hundred-percent smoke free, but not today at two nearby tables. A moment ago I started to write "it's noisy in here," thinking it a matter of conviviality on Christmas day in one of the only open places. Now, however, the sound is roaring up at me from a half-floor below. What must be a large family reunion is downright screaming and cheering some process along that seems to involve strumming a guitar and sports-arena-style chants. They are all very loud and mindless of others. Occasionally I hear "Silence" from another brave soul in the pub, but to no avail. Flashes from cameras click steadily, and now a young man is reading a long something as the guitar thrums. The others of us (who are with companions) now have a level of conversational music above which normal dialogue is audible. The man still reads. Maybe they are descendants of Picasso. The room explodes in "Bravo!" for the reader. The clapping is unceasing.

I realize I probably sound whiney, when really, it's impossible to have a bad day or night in Paris. I am currently finishing the carafe of Touraine Sauvignon which tastes mildly of apples and does not offend my naïve and unsuspecting palate. *Decà crème est arrivé.*

Now a little girl among that crowd is singing. Now an old lady. The rest of us hush a bit to listen. It's not lovely, but probably charming. She is still singing. It's a long sentence. It goes on. I catch the word "paradise." The room explodes again with cheers when she stops: *Rosette! Rosette! Rosette!* Then another little girl sings—when she stops even those up here cheer and clap, and the reunion folk pound the table deliriously. Now another little girl sings. What is going on? What an interesting tradition. No one seems to break out in tears at the idea of being on stage or at the thunderous applause. Now a little boy sings.

I've been here an hour. Daylight begins to fail, and I am getting very sick of the shouting.

December 26, 2007
Versailles

I'm in Café Richard outside the Versailles Palace. We will meet in ten minutes for the group tour (the bus ride was only about thirty minutes, so we're here early). I timed forty minutes walking from Hotel Monge to Cityrama tours (rue des Pyramides). Maybe I can avoid taxis in the future by sacrificing sleeping in.

☙

Yesterday after the pub, I stumbled right into the entrance of the Montmartre cemetery, after first going in the wrong direction. It was very different from how I imagined it last time: it actually appears as a village of above-ground tombs on cobblestone, tree-lined avenues. The scale is, of course, smaller. I never found Derrida or Stendhal, because I had to keep moving with the daylight waning.

I was not fast enough. I got very lost and turned around. After an hour of confusion and strong fatigue, I finally swallowed pride and took a taxi home. The good thing to come out of my taxi ride was a full conversation in French. We discussed the glorious view of the Champs at night, and I also learned of a place called "Paradise Latin"—which is, apparently, not to be missed. (What is it? Well, I didn't quite follow that part of the conversation.)

☙

Later I returned to Salon des Tartes. I am now sitting before a small carafe of Riesling and a vanished plate of spaghetti *aux fines herbes*, but I think it was only parsley. I am reminded that tossing anything in olive oil makes for a fine late lunch.

An extremely elegant lady in a fur coat, middle age, here with a dear friend (I assume by their long and animated conversation), just tapped me on the shoulder and gave me a really long compliment on my Ecuadorian sweater, with profuse apologies for interrupting my writing. I love this place. I just wish I had had a better reply than *merci, merci bien, merci,* said with what was, I'm sure, a goofy smile.

ॐ

I've now seen Marie Antoinette's bed and her monogram on the massive, heavily gilded mirror in the anteroom. I want to see Sofia Coppola's *Marie Antoinette* again. From there, we viewed the side door that led to an underground passage below the Hall of Mirrors, which, as we know, didn't ultimately lead to an escape. Apparently, at the border dressed as a peasant, Marie Antoinette spoke and someone recognized her voice, or her accent, and they were all arrested. Well, Louis XVI also gave someone a royal coin, which only royal people had. Her voice and his coin gave them all away.

Somewhere not far away—I've now seen that place, too—is where she was imprisoned, writing daily to her sons (who were in a different prison, but never executed, although perhaps starved to death). She was paying extra for a room with a window and, of course, the bribes to send the letters. Somewhere also near, which I've also seen, they cut off her head. She was only thirty-eight. The heart of one of the boys—presumably the dauphin, verified by DNA as one of the sons—is preserved and on display at a place of honor for kings and queens. He is such a beautiful six-year-old boy in the painting in her anteroom.

This trip has been less about Josephine and more about Marie Antoinette, from my reading not just *Annette Vallon* but also *Season of Upheaval*, a fabulously well-written account of the revolutions in America, France, and Russia. (Annette Vallon was Wordsworth's paramour and had a child with him. The story is very much a reprisal of *Gone with the Wind*, except Wordsworth was the faithless one. Besides that, Annette fended off the barbarous *sans-culottes*, though she was not entirely a royalist in her motivation to be in the underground movement. She did, however, wear their ribbons in a safe house, when a king returned to the throne—but before Napoleon. In the end she received land and a pension. I can't help but wonder if this tale, as told, is generally true. Dorothy Wordsworth does not come off well.) The age of Sun Kings ended fantastically bloody. I have decided it's better to be born now.

Listening to all of these guides and reading the histories, it occurs to me that Paris as it is today would be a very unfamiliar place to those whose names are on streets, squares, statues, and palaces. The guide said that Napoleon III actually laid out the city and the major avenues. He is much later than both Marie Antoinette and Josephine.

※

I'm now off to the Centre Pompidou in search of a fancy pen.

December 27, 2007
On a bus

I'm on the bus back to Paris from the Loire Valley. I'm actually very close to Blois (the setting of *Annette Vallon*), so one of the castles I've seen today must have been the model for the novel. I have been thrilled to see the small towns, churches, and the hunting woods in person. Now I have the details to completely fill in the backdrop of the story.

There has been a minor tragedy (in the scope of the trip): my camera is lost. I had it up until the third château. Then it was just gone. I am agonizing over whether to replace it and somehow retake my favorite Paris shots at least. The euro is so high right now that it discourages technological investments. It's now too bumpy, so I'll stop writing.

⁂

Salon des Tartes

To cope, let me write a list of photos that I'll never see again or ever get to show someone:

1. Pink clouds in blue sky just after Musée de l'Orangerie.
2. Musée de l'Orangerie from over the entrance.
3. The men outside that door who called to my attention that I'd dropped my shawl, the one Steve gave me years ago.
4. The full moon rising against bare trees of the Tuileries as I walked home from the museum.

5. The sign showing you where to plug in your electric car.

6. Chez les Filles restaurant interior: also Le Relais Gascon interior.

7. "Oscar de la Disco," written in neon, beneath a neon Coca-Cola sign.

8. The cab driver (in his rearview mirror) as I'd tried to photograph the Ferris wheel alit on the far end of the massively lighted Champs-Élysées.

9. Several photos of a mechanical "Marcel Marceau" mime in white face, but wearing a blue and white, wide-striped suit, who gave superb performance outside Centre Pompidou.

10. A short, pink, rectangular house so pale and unique— and I'd wanted to take a companion photo of another pink building I'd found.

11. "FRENCH FOOD," the infamous red neon sign framed in blue.

12. A beauty shop on Christmas Eve, in which a beautician was dressed as Santa Claus.

13. Lots in the Loire Valley (especially the woods), but the hunting dogs were especially surprising: regal, flawless, pure hunters, seemingly awaiting royal command still.

December 28, 2007
Le Carrousel, 7:20 a.m.

I am back here again, before the tour leaves. I have paid a fortune for scrambled eggs, but I take all of the remaining chunks of baguettes and the wrapped butter. Now I have something to get through the long day, remembering that the only provision yesterday was a poor lunch. Though the entrée and dessert were great, the main course was unbelievably banal, like eating a TV dinner, frozen then popped into a microwave. More on subject of yesterday's tour to come, but first I feel compelled to continue the list of lost images:

14. Two of myself smiling in the white, white bathroom, with the morning sun. It was very bright, I was in a white T-shirt trying to show the vast whiteness of that bathroom and the shock of the tiny red camera in all the white—oh, how I continue to mourn its loss.

15. The *presse* ("newsstand") where I bought a *Herald Tribune* the other day. The woman behind the little counter was enclosed in a collapsible stall, fitted with racks, with many loose racks around as well.

16. The St. Martin street sign.

17. The sign over the massive doors entering a ministry: "Ministère d' Encouragement," in large letters. In small letters below that: "Industrie Dévelopment."

18. Three story-high black-and-white photographs on the way to Centre Pompidou, each of a different older man with a funny expression on his face: the middle one was making a big rounded "O" with his mouth.

19. A full, life-size replica of Batman flying overhead in the
store where I got Otto a 500-page cartoon book of Teen
Titans. (Otto told me on Christmas Day that he
thought his dad would like it, too.)

❧

I have now completed my first champagne-maker tour and tast-
ing: Mumm & Co. I chose a delicious semi-brut, though I was in
the minority as the rest wanted brut. Incidentally, that's all that
was available in the quarter-*bouteille*, which I have purchased for
my personal New Year's celebration.

Everyone has a camera today, and all they do (the Lyonese) is
take each other's picture every few steps. Without a camera I am
freer to float along—which is a preferred state—but I must try to
imprint my memory with the red-ribbon emblem of Mumm &
Co. and a purple door on one of the houses in town.

Coming this way, we passed a display of the old devices and
equipment used for making champagne, accompanied by old
photos of workers using them. It made me think that all shop
floors look similar, and did even over a hundred years ago—the
image is one of many human beings doing work that someone
else designed.

It's still a gray day at half past eleven, so I'm not imagining
much change, but at least it's not raining.

❧

I'm reading *The Elephanta Suite* by Paul Theroux. I have chosen
Theroux again because I feel we both harbor a (sometimes) very

dark understanding of people. The difference is I would never have the courage to say or write it, whereas he shamelessly draws the Indian figure, as seen and experienced by the ugly American couple, as well as his view of them. No one comes across as beneficent, holy, good, well-intentioned, honest, or mentally well—on either the individual or cultural level. There is a raging determinism in his work, of which the human ego is the driving force. This will to pretension and self-consciousness draws the character deeper into an abyss of extreme ignorance. Only the reader can "see" their true direction. They believe they are headed for redemption (not unlike finding myself on the rue Sebastopol in the belief that I'm headed toward Sacré-Cœur). His prose and the terror evoked at the moments of destruction (does the character ever learn anything? nothing in the detail suggests it) are riveting and provocative in the ultimate sense. To me, Theroux is like Joseph Conrad on steroids.

To think I was worried about how my hair would look growing out.

❧

Yesterday at nine at night, after my late arrival from the Loire Valley, I feasted on French fries and French mayo again at the Salon. I also ate chicken roasted with white sweet potatoes in a dish.

❧

The French countryside was in deep, white fog for my second champagne tour, Moët, which was very pleasing overall. This time, I must try to remember the image of a human-sized ice sculpture of a champagne bottle at the entrance.

I was most impressed with the elegant tour guide. I want to be her, beginning with her perfect skin and thin build. Her short haircut framed the fine bones in her face. I couldn't help but notice that the irises of her beautiful eyes were fully round (not occluded, as mine have become) and her teeth were perfect. She dressed superbly in a black suit, with a black and tan, patterned scarf so expertly tied, and red nails. The entire effect was very poised: she wore a large black stone set in a silver ring on her middle finger. It was so elegant, balanced, unfussy, yet ring, scarf, earrings, make-up, and the draped shawl she wore when we went into the "caves" tied together. How did she do it? What I admired and envied most was her lovely, soothing Princess Diana voice saying, after a detailed explanation of double fermentation: "Is that okay? Would you care to follow me to the next step?" She used exact terms. I struggle to recall the one that means "fizzes up the wine." She, I hope, is actually a countess, slumming as a champagne tour guide to polish up the brand favored by Napoleon. I found it endearing when she said "Napoleon the First." Would anyone be confused, really, if she'd left off "the first"?

December 29, 2007
On a bus

I'm now on the bus, still across from the breakfast bistro where I paid $16 for scrambled eggs, toast, juice, and *decà crème* again—because they give baguette chunks upon request, which I put in a little plastic bag, with the butter, for later. (Did I already write about this? I'm reminded that not only forgetting, but also repeating oneself, is associated with Alzheimer's, one of my main fears in aging. I will admit one purpose of recounting the lost photos was to prove, again, that I still have all the faculties of a normal person of my age, and I'm overall mentally intact. (Shades of *Exit Ghost*.)

☙

Remember Epernay—the second stop after Rheims and the champagne district.

December 30, 2007
Petit déjeuner at the hotel

The bus pulled away, and from that point there was no opportunity to write. That trip was indeed an experience, more about being a tall, white, older woman surrounded by young, Japanese girls in baby-doll outfits endlessly giggling and unchecked by their reserved and unsmiling parents. I felt being surrounded by their apparent insularity brought out a deep streak of selfishness, my own generous side being not overly big to begin with. Can you imagine standing in line more than thirty minutes, tourists in queue ahead and behind as far as you can see? If it weren't for wanting to see Eleanor of Aquitaine's destination quite so much, I might have walked away and thought "never again" with the tours.

Epernay was memorable. I think I was going to comment, but the point escapes me at the moment. ("Red, red wine . . . ," the reggae song, is playing now. I've neglected to note the soundtrack very much this trip.)

Mont St. Michel was the most satisfying experience of the day for several reasons. First, picturing the great and long-lasting queen Eleanor was deeply compelling. I imagined her presence along the way. While many details on the surface must be totally different, surely it must be a same experience for the senses. For that reason, I relished the climb to such great heights in the darkness, buffeted by sea breezes, and standing at various places in the cloisters. Was she barred from the monks' private spaces, or was her divine right greater than theirs? It felt a little bit anti-divine to see all of us (may I add, all of us Japanese—I being an exceptionally small or negligible percentage of the demographic totals) tramping about noisily. There we were, using un-divine digital flashes at even uninteresting objects, usually with an un-divine tot held up in front of a minor archway. We continued, trampling on the once-hallowed stones in the church, the dormitory, the refractory, the cloisters, the scriptorium, the ossuary, the royal receiving rooms (tapestries gone now and only fake candles), and the receiving rooms for regular pilgrims. Last was the room where beggars, if they survived the trip across the low-tide quicksand, were received and given food.

We pilgrims were all given an *omelette de la Mère Poulard*. The dish is named for Mère Poulard, a relatively recent inhabitant who became legendary for always managing to find eggs on "the rock" to make omelets. Again we had the pressed turkey (which must be a tour standard) and a tasty dessert they called cheesecake but was actually a round, stubby cylinder of sweet curd. We drank a strong cider that tasted more like beer than anything else.

I learned that "Normandy" comes from "north man's land," referring to the Swedish, who won wars with the French in early times. I bought a primer on French history so that all these new exposures to the past could come into better focus. It seems there were plenty of times that this country could have become, for example, English, Islamic, or Spanish.

∽

It seems that my hotel is under new ownership and is to be renamed Hotel Acte V. The future of this hotel—will I want to continue coming here? Act V, the final act of a play, right? Hmmm.

❧

Now here is a saga worth telling: that of how I bought another Nikon without the anxiety of waiting beyond Sunday (today) when stores would be closed (so I imagined). I mentioned at the end of the Champagne tour to the tour guide that the previous day my camera went missing. I was standing in line at the agency trying to see if my Mt. St. Michel trip could be rescheduled, to give me Saturday to find a camera. She suggested a shop two blocks away that processed film: "They might sell cameras." So off I went only to find they do not sell cameras, but the young man was sympathetic, and wrote out directions for riding the Metro to FNAC on the Champs-Élysées (which was actually where I had imagined I'd start the search).

The Metro is a fearsome challenge to a sense of competence. I really wanted to go camera shopping, however, without having to contend with the "open/closed" Sunday challenge. So with heavy bags from souvenirs on my arms, and very tired from the all-day tour, I set off for the Metro. The crowds were unbelievable. Head down, I plowed through it all, found a line for tickets, found the change to buy a one way (I was unable to communicate the concept of "round trip"), and followed instructions. I won't bore you with other exciting details related to being misdirected twice (I hadn't thought to ask where on the Champs FNAC was, and so found myself quite lost on the long, two-sided boulevard which was packed to the max with frantic holiday tourists of all kinds). At last I arrived at the camera section of FNAC, where I found that my little red Nikon had been "sold out," as signified by the sign on the display. I asked a young and very reserved nerd at the

Help Desk nearby if he could help, to which he demonstrated probably not but he'd try. He confirmed the sold status and recommended a Fuji as a very similar model. I went for the next level-up Nikon instead, and he smiled. It came in a complete package with charger, memory card, and carrying case, the works. I also smiled. I didn't have to go to seven places in the camera section to buy all of these items, as I would have at Best Buy. Can you imagine my sense of competence after all of this? Not to mention I got back on the Metro, back to the hotel, opened the package only to find the manual was in every language except English (it was on a CD), and still, less than a hundred minutes later, I was taking pictures with a fully charged Nikon Cool Pix digital camera (granted, not red, but working). I've now retaken "FRENCH FOOD," "Oscar de la Disco," clouds in Normandy (not soft pink, but pretty dramatic anyway), and today offers a chance to continue my "recovery of the past," even if the past was only a week ago.

❧

Another small but meaningful triumph: I asked one of the hotel girls if newsstands were open on Sunday, because I had wanted the weekend edition of *The Herald Tribune* and was unable to get it yesterday. She told me they are closed everywhere except at railroad stations and that she would show me the nearest one on the map. Then, offhandedly, she asked what I intended to buy. "*The Herald Tribune*," I said. "Oh!" she said and went across the street to another hotel and came back with a copy. I saved two euros and twenty cents, but that's not the point. I'm fascinated by the idea that you can just put what you need out there and somehow it arrives.

In the paper, I discovered that Benazir Bhutto was killed two days ago, at the age of fifty-four. She was an icon in Pakistan. I had heard an old interview of her on NPR just a couple of weeks ago, a piece done while she was under house arrest. I was listening while following my usual routine then. I was scheduling myself to wake up at five, walk from quarter past five to quarter past six, bathe, dress, review the day's obligations, wash clothes, and make the bed, all while hearing the vivid news of the day, that of a younger woman determined to put herself in the path of a violent death. It was a miracle that she had not been killed already.

☙

I set out in a totally different direction today, searching for a production of *Piaf, Une Vie en Rose et Noir*, and found a whole new Paris world. If I'd known about the huge open market on rue Richard Lenoir, I would have saved all my souvenir shopping for this place. I bought five silk/pashmina shawls for only twenty euros, even though I'd already bought nine. Also, after an inventory of clothes came up short, I bought two warm tops.

Stoic me: after I noticed a bit of weight gain despite the many daily miles, I threw away the hoarded baguette pieces. I also swore off pastries and French fries with mayo. Tough.

I have now stopped at a Chinese restaurant, out of curiosity and in need of a restroom. I still haven't navigated all of Voltaire Boulevard, but the day is yet young and sunny. It is actually quiet and surprisingly elegant in here. Three elderly and well-appointed women are meeting for lunch. They kiss cheeks, smile shaky smiles, and turn around very slowly to get situated at the table. Only one has gray hair showing. Their high, tremulous voices begin. The shrimp-in-curry soup with rice noodles is delicious but needs to cool off. I observe that the clientele is from the neighborhood and generally quite elderly. They all know the proprietor. There are no other tourists; outside, I saw joggers for the first time. So I am clearly in a different Paris atmosphere, but there are still the grand monuments around, most notably the Bastille. You'd think the Bastille prison of all things would have been preserved, but now it's an opera house: so Mont St. Michel had been a monastery and then became a prison while the Bastille had been a prison and now becomes an opera house. It's some form of evolution, certainly, but what kind? Regardless, both are now places where the masses congregate of their own free will.

ↀ

It's been an interesting day. It's seven in the evening and completely dark. I'm at the Salon des Tartes now. I have finished the spinach and goat cheese tart and the blackberry one (it's the deal: two *tartes* for nine euros) and am sipping on the Riesling and thinking of the *decà crème* to come. The indulgence is to make up for two disappointments—one being that when I opened my bag at the end of the long walking adventure in the new side of Paris, I found only four, not five, scarves. I had miscounted because of the folds—rats. The second disappointment was finding out later in the day, while retracing the path to Cirque d'Hiver, that the Edith Piaf show would not play again until January.

The triumph was that I finally found the venue, not once but twice, and I was really captivated by that grand voice coming out of the tiny person who played Piaf in *La Vie en Rose*. What a spectacular experience. Maybe next time I will figure out two things: how to get to Dreux and how to attend a live performance. Another triumph—no bleeding feet and toes. I broke my strong rule about dressing like an ugly American and wore my Nikes both today and yesterday, and they—my feet—have rewarded me by not bleeding and hurting. At least they are my cool Nikes: black with silver trim.

Other rules, which will not be broken, include: no jeans, sweatpants, or sweatshirts, and nothing that screams I-am-American-and-therefore-unwilling-to-accept-that-my-comfy/casual-look-offends-the-world. Another rule—don't consume anything from the little fridge—go out and get something tasty across the street. More rules to be kept include: an airborne tablet dissolved in warm water every morning, a scarf every day (try to tie it correctly). Also, unless on tour, sleep in and come back midday if I want and squander the little daylight afforded in December by reading novels or sleeping again. Another: I wrote the Amex international customer service number on a post-it, and I wear it in my bra in case my purse or credit cards are stolen, or in case the card demagnetizes and I can't get cash. (Amex will send a one-time, emergency credit of five hundred dollars.) Also: as many bubble baths per day as needed. Usually only one, but, in case . . . just do it. And: don't worry about anything. Keep walking and see what turns up. For example, I found out today that new Paris meets old Paris at St. Antoine and Tivoli. Who knew?

All of this has made me settle down and stop "scheduling" myself so totally, which I do at home where there is never enough time to just think and, if desired, listen to the radio or meditation CDs or just spend time thinking about nothing in particular. Here, all the new keeps shuttling me from thought to thought to thought, pierced only occasionally by the habit acquired to check: "Are my wallet, Blackberry, camera, passport in view? If not, put current activity on hold until they are."

Here I can write something down every day. Most recently I copy: "Savage with health, and armed to the teeth with time," Philip Roth, *Exit Ghost*. I imagine that if I'd done this kind of daily writing as a means of conjuring up conversation with someone, even if just myself, maybe by age seventy-seven I, too, would be writing such devastating lines as these. I watch my pen continue to fly across this page. I am alive enough.

☙

The young woman inches away to take a photo of her white tureen of soup with her phone. I'd do the same thing. It proves something, doesn't it? I'd like to think of my documentation as somehow more respectable than the hoards I visited *Mont St. Michel* with. It's endlessly entertaining to watch passing clusters of people arrive at the menu posted by the door and discuss the merits of entering. I always mentally encourage them to come on in. I am wearing not one but two Austrian crystal rings today, and they sparkle with greater radiance in this indoor light than they do in the sun. By the way, I found that the Centre Pompidou was closed before not because it was Christmas but because it was Tuesday. They always close on Tuesday. The young girl scrapes the tureen for the last drop. I'd do the same.

December 31, 2007
Indian restaurant off Mouffetard

It's two in the afternoon, and I'm the only one here. A tall, congenial young waiter took my order, and I managed to order regular tap water incorrectly, so now I have a huge bottle of water in front of me. I'm close to the hotel, so maybe today is about staying close to home base, or perhaps just drinking a lot of water. I slept late this morning, had a croissant and *decà crème* but left the extra bread and all the butter and cheese, hoping for a more virtuous day. Then I took a long, hot bubble bath after sorting out how all the souvenirs correspond to friends and family and which of the remaining clothes were clean vs. needing to be washed. I have repacked everything and I note that the suitcase is full—that is, the one I brought completely empty for which I received a comment from the rep at the international counter: "Going shopping?"

The plan after my leisurely morning was to buy a newspaper, then find a laundromat, which offered a potentially fresh experience in all senses. I had my doubts, however, about whether I could do it without ending up with a huge pile of dirty clothes and no underwear when I got home. I found a newspaper easily enough, and to my surprise the search for a laundromat was blessedly short. I was surprised, however, to find how one does laundry in a French laundromat—it was not intuitive or obvious. The whole place is computer-managed from a *centrale*, or cabinet that takes your machine number then accepts your coins, which may buy soap, wash time, or dry time. Thank goodness two non-French women were there to explain the process. It resulted in another triumphant moment as I left an hour later with clean clothes and much of the Monday puzzles done.

I returned to my room to leave the clean laundry and then came time to answer the wonderful question: which direction today? The answer was: back on the street to find this Indian place. The vegetable samosa, curry, and the sweet at the end have all been just delicious, bringing to mind why the spice trade must have been one of the earliest drivers of commerce: "I want that curry again," thought the Queen.

These little ethnic restaurants always seem to have friends and family coming and going, clustering in the back rooms and talk-ing, laughing, and talking some more. The people working are so terribly kind while waiting on me. They always spot me as non-native, however, and they never understand my French, which is just the most basic. So I have concluded I have an accent, which should be no surprise, but I was still clinging to some hope. Mme Julie always complimented me on my pronunciation, so, I thought maybe . . .

Oh, good, the bottle has no label. It's just a carafe that had a past life with a label, but today is used to serve regular water. What a relief; I'll stop trying so hard to drink it all. It must be the equivalent of five or six glasses of water.

∾

Elephanta Suite has been haunting to read—so desperately draw-ing between dark and darker. I can't wait to read a critical analysis or two on Theroux. I'll bet it's not easy to name the essential oppositions, but they are definitely there, all of them—struggle, exploitation, fake redemption, fake joy, fake success, and a pervasive knowingness in the tone. It reads like Roth, like Updike, like Bellow, with such power and energy created with words.

ↄ

It's now going on eight o'clock. After a nap, I decided just to wander in the general direction of St. Germaine by way of des Écoles, the Sorbonne area, maybe on to the Champs-Élysées to watch the more experienced revelers enjoy New Year's Eve (called *réveillon*, as I learned at a shop on rue Mouffetard). In the process, the sun went down, and I walked and walked, bought lotion, walked more, all the while dreading to go without a net (no map, no sense of where each changing block was going to finally dump me out).

I experienced a strange feeling, best described as "nonplussed" I think, from finding the ideal gifts, clearly superior to the choices I made, on these streets tonight when it is too late to change anything. Theo, for example, asked for so little: "colorful tennis shoes"—and I walked right past a shop full of them. Then there were the orange pens, Parker no less, on sale, but the money had been spent already. One of the rules, I decide, is not to let nonplussed become chagrin or frustration or irritation on any level. It is a universal concept that the tourist is by definition unable to buy things of the preferred style, price, or convenience. If you were to be able to have all that, it would be unnatural.

Another old rule that bears repeating: take a perfume and use it daily without fail. It not only comforts you as predictable reassurance of yourself; it also will bring back memories years in the future, should you come across that fragrance. I brought Elizabeth Arden Green Tea to use up on this trip alone. I'm formulating a new rule at home: use up all the many bottles of perfume with little amounts remaining, so that by the age of sixty-five I can perhaps settle once and for all on one fragrance, which today would be a toss-up between Chanel No. 5 and one by Esteé Lauder, which I think is called Youth Dew.

∾

I'm at Salon des Tartes for my New Year's Eve meal. *Tarte myrtille* ("blueberry") is my dessert—*boeuf* was my *plat*. I should have known it would be ground beef, but it was so good it saved me from any disappointment. I'm drinking the Riesling again, and shortly I will have my *decà crème*.

I watch the people come to the outside menu and observe how hard it is to make decisions when there is more than one person studying the options: there's much back and forth, then re-examining, then stepping back and weighing (as others approach the same crossroads). Sometimes an argument results, sometimes revisiting two or three times. I see a boy and girl who appear so earnest—why are they struggling so much to decide? A stout woman in a red coat with a very short woman in a white one—both older than I—really expend themselves on whether to come in. They don't. Now, two more approach. They read, review, retreat. Did I already mention how ludicrously pervasive the Burberry plaid has become? Old men. Small dogs, babies in strollers—where, or on whom, will it end?

∾

I have discovered such vastly differing views on Bhutto's death between *The Herald Tribune* and *The Observer* (another English paper). In one, it's hailed as a tragic event; in the other the sentiment "she had it coming" prevails. It all reminds me of the Indira Gandhi moment and how our institutions revere and cling to dynasties in crises. It makes you ask, "What is really happening here?" The culture and sense of the question has changed since Dylan so effectively posed the same question, but I think some of the underlying factors remain the same.

We may be closer to "one world" thinking than ever, just a pendulum swing away, but not in my lifetime. Maybe in Otto's or Emory's, as they move across continents to work and play, side by side with people who speak different languages, eat different cuisines, and have different customs, but who will assert their equality until it becomes their right. I read today, for instance, that Europe has not supported the Iraq war because too many of their workers are Muslim. The result of their loss would be declining birthrates and therefore a gaping hole in the economic structures that keep the culture alive. Most western countries have this phenomenon and are not reconciled to the idea of sharing, yet are unable to say "no" to the rising tides of immigrants (legal or not). To me, this all signifies that the melting pot is occurring on a global scale.

☙

So funny, the couple who deliberated so many times has finally come inside—they're American and both have ordered French fries, in the same way that I did one time here, with the same semi-brave French. My French has become a little braver, on a scale, so to speak. Six Americans, raw boned, plain, overweight, and seemingly of a religious tour group, have come in and elevated the sound level. They also order French fries.

The whole restaurant has filled up in the last ten minutes—my Austrian crystal rings twinkle.

Being alone is such an interesting phenomenon. Every second of my two weeks in Paris seems to stand out in contrast to the unmarked day-to-day passage of time at home. So far I feel incapable of living an empty or boring day here. My mind feels properly balanced between familiar and fearsomely unfamiliar, tied together by a desire to make it all familiar and wear down any frightening foreignness, but there is always more that is mystifying. Today really had the least concept of purpose or destiny, yet my feeling here, now going on nine at night, is that the possibilities of thought and observation are infinite.

I order *decà crème* and decide to put the teensy square of chocolate into the cup. Hope it does not ruin the treat. In fact, the melting chocolate works well, making the coffee slightly more bitter, but in a New Year's Eve sort of way.

As I reflect on the now-institution Les Deux Magots, I ponder how it is that a café gets selected by the terribly wonderful sensibilities of the age so that about fifty years later the place can become a mecca. Anyway, I would easily choose this place, it is so conducive to *joie* just being here, near the ancient and the modern. The food is excellent and more or less affordable. While the staff are not quite endearing, because they don't know who you are, they're close enough. I'm also convinced that if I actually lived here and chose this as my café for writing and meeting my colleagues, endearing would naturally follow.

A very interesting couple has come in, sitting where the girl photographed her soup bowl yesterday. The woman is my age, with long, flowing hair and a sweet face. She is wearing a total of six silver rings on surprisingly massive hands. The man, also about my age, sports a nineteenth-century mustache. They are both slender and conservatively dressed. Perhaps, they are brother and sister. They study the menu and make quiet comments. They are French. Maybe she is younger than I am; maybe she is really blond.

I do the tourist thing of taking a picture of the left side of the restaurant, then one in front of me, to capture the table where I normally am seated, or at least where I am offered, as it has become "my table." Today, however, others were already there when I came in.

I note that the intense emotional state I was in when I came in has passed. I was almost in tears without being sure of the cause of the emotions. I assume they were partly related to the long conversation I had with Steve in which he expressed frustration with my poor computer systems. He compared it to the feelings we both share when we find earnest operators struggling with poor equipment—a touching rage on my behalf made me weepy as I walked, somewhat lost, on Montparnasse. Coming into this favorite place to have supper and being greeted by a kind person who recognizes me ("she will order something different from before but maybe with another carafe of Riesling") brought the emotions back. The feelings are not at all of a soul alone, then, but of a soul well loved but feeling undeserving.

Well, which way to go? Home or Tuileries? I think home, back to the little champagne bottle, the rest of *Elephanta Suite*, and to sleep.

January 1, 2008
Café de la Place

Sitting at breakfast, forced to drink hot chocolate because the decaf machine was broken, I read my *Paris Guide* in an attempt to understand last night's wanderings. I found, to my amazement, that I was only steps away from things I have often pondered. They included not only the cemetery but also La Coupole, a Hemingway haunt Gwen took us to. The purpose of the day then became to return to this area with a better sense of direction. So I headed out for Montparnasse Cemetery.

I came upon the Closerie de Lilas on today's walk, where the guide says Hemingway wrote *The Sun Also Rises* in six weeks on the terrace. Now, according to the menu out front, the place is quite expensive. The doormen in gray suits also seemed hired to look very judgmental. Though I am not wearing my Nikes today, I assume I probably still wouldn't be ushered in. So I took a photo (with a camera that now has an incredibly tight security wristband).

On the way to the cemetery I also saw a poster announcing a three-day conference on Beauvoir in honor of her would-be hundredth birthday, being put on by Julia Kristeva, whom I "met" in Chicago at an event with Derrida. I gave her an AT&T pen, and she signed her book for me, which I came across again when moving. I had thought it was lost, since I'd wanted to give it to Nat for a birthday present a few years ago and could not find it. At times Paris seems to make coincidences from my memories.

It's now about half past one in the afternoon, and I'm a block from the Montparnasse Cemetery, which I have just left, in a little café waiting for onion soup to arrive. Inside I found Sartre and Beauvoir immediately. Pink petals from shrubs outside made a bed on which Simone de Beauvoir's simple grave seemingly rested. If I'd understood the map to begin with, I'd also have found Baudelaire right away. Instead, I spent ages reading amazingly indecorous tombs.

Finally, when I was almost fed up with looking for Baudelaire, a petite woman my age wearing altogether stylish and refined glasses and brown suede boots, came up to me and asked in French whether I knew where to find him. When she learned we were on the same quest, she asked to see my map (given at the entrance), and by her analysis I observed how the map works. Together we found him. We exchanged a few comments relating to the inscription—then I saw her again at Beckett. We were clearly destined to be friends.

I found Beckett, whose tomb was as plain as that of Beauvoir; both are so unlike the elaborate apartments that enclose everyone else. I couldn't help but take a lot of photographs. Unfortunately, however, I couldn't find Man Ray, even after understanding the map code. For a cemetery, it was full of life. The place was brimming with "informal" Christmas trees and Metro tickets at the celebrity tombs along with all kinds of other flotsam you would expect to find at an endless funeral: photos, flowers, and framed letters of sorrow.

✑

I found the Luxembourg Gardens at a great time for a winter day. I sit at a chess table set as part of a permanent row of five. I take a photo of a father and daughter playing chess and next to them, a pair of young men who play fast and slap a sort of timer box one after the other, or is it a timer box? What is that thing? I imagine this place in the spring and already want to return.

There are many young fathers with children and many more pigeons. The sun comes out slightly, for the first time in a week. I have not able to retake the happy white bathroom photo, yet, and am still waiting for that radiant moment. I continue to observe. Some people are living, walking works of art.

January 2, 2008
Au General Lafayette

It's one in the afternoon, and there's a little sun today. I've found a quicker way to get to Montmartre, but where the scene gets a little more ragged, as it did with Sebastopol, the atmosphere is more Bourbon Street without the bars. Instead, a more artsy appeal extends to endless *salons de thé*, restaurants, little walk-in-closet grocery stores, and wine shops. A mix of many nationalities blends on the sidewalks, standing at the corners and dashing in front of each other.

I decided on having a worry-free day again, to balance old with new, and to stop for lunch and tea whenever I felt like it, although I did not want to have a really heavy meal until a last dinner at Salons des Tartes, planning to be totally worn out by then and ready for good sleep. I've already packed everything, checked the shuttle confirmation, and have about eighty euros to spend. So, I return to finish the climb to Sacré-Cœur, and intend to fix all the streets and turns in my memory by writing them down.

On my way, I was in front of Notre Dame at noon, when all hell broke loose with the bells. Somehow in all these visits I've never been here at bell time. They rang for over ten minutes. It was astonishing, that they should continue in that way through history. Bemused, I decided to try something new: just past the cathedral I had a sweet crepe with lemon hot off a street skillet. It delighted my whole being, which by then had begun to notice the bitter cold and knew that the walk ahead would be rough and long. For the first stop, I chose a bistro called Au General Lafayette. I had onion soup again, again good, and chef salad, which was mostly potato salad with all the usual ingredients plus big slabs of awful-tasting chicken. I added a small carafe of white wine in honor of this, my last day.

I am just about to leave; however, a scholar has joined another scholar at the table next to me. They are both men and American. I quickly decide to linger a few minutes and listen in on their conversation. The older one comes across as a busy, busy author, an academic of a familiar type. Apparently he has a book coming out in March. It's clear that both have experienced setbacks of a somewhat humiliating nature, by the way they so tenderly explain their circumstances and tiptoe around their need to get something from each other. It's not hard to see through the posturing and stroking, being superior and patronizing. They're clearly trying to disguise a failure, a weakness, or an uncertainty of some kind. The younger one, the conversation reveals, has been rebuffed by someone who knew, or was related to, Franco. He has just arrived from Madrid looking for new contacts: "I had it all lined up, but all of a sudden no one can be found." Long pause.

"Well," the other says and encourages without conviction and says he "can't guarantee anything," but without suggesting he is actually without any of the necessary relationships. The older man, admitting more of his failed circumstances, concludes: "Well, and I am in Paris after all for another two months," a consolation anyone could understand. I wonder what his book is about. What is left to be said about Franco? The younger scholar used the phrase "super fascist," which didn't have a ring of authenticity; maybe he was just trying to put the older scholar at ease by not over-playing his ambition. He clearly needed the older one.

❧

While *Annette Vallon* was certainly a fortuitous novel to be reading when visiting the Loire Valley, my current reading list has diverged quite dramatically. Now that I have finished *Elephanta Suite*, I am immersed in *Half a Yellow Sun*, which Steve Waltingham sent me, following our tradition of exchanging novels every year. This story is about the dissolution of Nigeria in the sixties and the creation of Biafra, basically tribes slaughtering one another. In this novel, as with most of the novels I've read set in Africa, the story carries an underlying thesis that many of the problems in Africa stem from Westerners' ignorance and cruelty, which leads to a decidedly anti-Western influence and power. It's really interesting stuff and in its own way apropos of what's going on in France and in the world these days. In fact, this week's headlines are almost identical to the events behind the novel, except the massacres are in Kenya instead of Nigeria.

❧

I am at Montmartre at last; it is mid-afternoon, and sun is bright. Not surprisingly, it's clearly the place to be today. In the crowd are lots of couples kissing (all ages) with everyone getting their portrait done or profile cut out (what an interesting art form). *Sacré-Cœur* and the square of pop art are so opposite in scale and aim, yet they combine somehow, if in a way that's slightly dizzying.

I did light another candle for my company, this time not out of desperation, but more in the hope that it remains real enough so that it can change and survive. Afterward, I decided to enter

Bohème du Tertre Café, which is jammed to the max with tourists. I have ordered tea for the first time on this trip, but the real reason I'm here is that I needed a restroom and peace to write a few more remarks. I'm feeling smug, meanwhile, that I found a new and better way to get here. I won't get lost or need a taxi home.

ও

"*Bizzoo, Bizzoo, Bizzoo, Martine!*" This is what I heard at the checkout counter a short while ago, on rue Monge, coming back from a long, cold, steep decline. I stopped in to stock up on tangerines, apples, and bananas, mainly for the flight home tomorrow. The woman near the counter was not quite elderly, but getting there. I saw her frown over something and look at her watch. She then called someone on a cell phone, talked pointedly and ended with the *bizzoos*. I think she was saying "*Bijoux, bijoux, bijoux.*" (Doesn't that mean kisses, kisses, kisses?)

Just before I got to the fruit section, I also passed the proprietor of Salon des Tartes in the aisle. We both did a double take and smiled. When I arrived at the restaurant for my last dinner out, he asked me if I live on this street now, and I told him no, but I'm staying in a nearby hotel, and that this was my last night before going back to the U. S. He insisted on giving me a glass of wine "*comme cadeau.*" So, just as I did two years ago, I left with a kind and friendly gesture. I promise myself I'll always come here when and if I visit Paris.

ও

I meant to comment throughout this journal that there is not the slightest pain in my hands or in any joints. I remember last time my right hand was in agony when trying to use a pen. I've put in a minimum of five miles per day and surely seven on a day like today, up a "mount" no less, but nothing hurts (except my pride that I've probably gained weight rather than lost it—could it possibly be the daily croissants, *tartes*, spaghetti, *croque monsieurs*, *crêpes*, French fries, wine, and baguettes with cheese?). For all of my rules, I have utterly smashed a few while at it, which has probably made the trip more fun, and definitely tastier. At least I know what to do about it when I get back.

Steve told me on the phone to suck the marrow out of the last day here. So I stopped to get a rhubarb *tarte* at the *patisserie* around the corner, and it turned out to be the best I've had anywhere, even here. It was very tart, and I plan to eat it late tonight on the assumption that I'll be what I've heard called "travel proud," unable to sleep given the anticipation of the big journey ahead.

Finis

A Note on the Type

This book is set in Adobe Garamond Pro, a digital typeface based on the type of Claude Garamond (c. 1480–1561). A native of Paris, Garamond was a publisher, type designer, and punch cutter whose typefaces are noted for their elegance.